CHEROKEE VOICES

*Early Accounts of
Cherokee Life in the East*

❧··❧

ALSO BY VICKI ROZEMA

Footsteps of the Cherokees:
A Guide to the Eastern Homelands of the Cherokee Nation

CHEROKEE VOICES

Early Accounts of Cherokee Life in the East

John F. Blair, Publisher ➤◄ Winston-Salem, North Carolina

Published by John F. Blair, Publisher

The paper in this book meets the guidelines
for permanence and durability of the
Committee on Production Guidelines for
Book Longevity of the Council on Library Resources

Image on front cover—
Scyacust Ukah, 1762, by Joshua Reynolds,
Oil on canvas, 0176.1017, from the Collection of Gilcrease Museum, Tulsa

Library of Congress Cataloging-in-Publication Data

Cherokee voices: early accounts of Cherokee life in the east / [compiled] by Vicki
Rozema.
      p.   cm.—(Real voices, real history series)
Includes bibliographical references and index.
   ISBN 0-89587-270-6 (alk. paper)
   1. Cherokee Indians—History. 2. Cherokee Indians—History—Sources. I. Rozema,
Vicki, 1954— II. Series.
   E99.C5 C6525 2002
   975.004'9755—dc21
                        2002010737

Book design by Debra Long Hampton

For my parents, Robert Thayer and Margaret Lois Brown Bell

CONTENTS

PREFACE

Of the many books about the Cherokees, the vast majority have been written in the third person by people who lived years after the events occurred. Old records are pulled from archives, dusted off, interpreted, and published by historians and writers who seek to peel back the layers of time to provide insights into our past. Regardless of how accurately they try to represent the events and people that shaped our country and our heritage, modern writers inevitably lose something in the translation of voices speaking from a different culture, a different time, and a different perspective. No one can speak more eloquently of their lives, trials, and customs than the people who actually lived the experiences.

This book is a collection of first-person accounts of the Cherokees during the eighteenth and nineteenth centuries. These selections have been gathered from journals, treaty records, and correspondence written by Cherokees or by Europeans or Americans who lived among or visited the Cherokees. The excerpts chosen represent a wide range of historical events and daily activities of the Cherokees. From the descriptions of treaty meetings, dances, sports, religion, and death, we witness a rich cultural tradition through the eyes of those who actually lived the events. Accounts of the 1838 Cherokee Removal are not included in this volume. The events surrounding the Trail of Tears are sufficient in scope to warrant a separate book, to follow shortly.

It is unfortunate that most of what we know about the Cherokees prior to the twentieth century was written by people of European descent. For this reason, I chose many of the accounts in this volume because they were written or spoken by Cherokees. I selected accounts in which the main speakers are white because they include speeches by Cherokees or provide unusual insight into the daily lives and customs of the Cherokees.

The accounts span nearly two centuries of Cherokee history and provide a glimpse of how Cherokee culture changed during that time period. They are arranged in chronological order starting with Alexander Cuming's visit in 1730, in which we see Cherokees from the Lower and Middle Settlements who are somewhat mesmerized by the British. Just twenty years later, we have a front-row seat at talks in Charleston, where skilled negotiators Little Carpenter and Skiagunsta argue successfully with the British governor for concessions and a new fort in the Cherokee Nation. The accounts take us from a period when the Cherokees were heavily dependent on European trade to a time when they became self-sufficient farmers, mechanics, and ferry operators. We watch as they change from an oral-bound tradition to a society publishing its own newspaper. We listen as they plead for the white man to leave their lands alone.

In an effort to be as fair to the original speakers as possible, I have chosen to edit the first-person accounts sparingly. Readers will encounter misspellings, poor grammar and punctuation, and inconsistencies of various sorts. But even in the least sophisticated of the narratives included here, strong and clear testimonies shine through.

In the eighteenth and early nineteenth centuries, handwriting and printing used the elongated *s*, which looks like a modern-day *f*. To avoid confusion in the accounts written prior to 1818, it was necessary to replace the elongated *s* with a standard *s*. In the excerpt from Alexander Cuming's journal in "Hands and Hearts Joined Together," I have removed paragraph numbers for readability. I performed additional editing on the chapter entitled "The Price of a White Shirt" to correct gross misspellings and some errors in capitalization and punctuation. In the section entitled "List of the Prices of Goods," I edited abbreviations and inserted explanations in brackets to clarify archaic terms. Finally, I found it necessary to greatly edit both of the Brainerd Mission letters in the chapter entitled "An Ardent Zeal" to make them readable. The Catharine Brown letter was particularly hard to read, due to its deteriorating condition, misspellings, and unusual punctuation. In each case, I have tried to leave colloquialisms, local vernacular, and the original meaning intact.

Many thanks are due the librarians and staffs at the Chattanooga-Hamilton County Bicentennial Library and the Lupton Library at the University of Tennessee at Chattanooga for their help while

I was researching this book. In addition, I would like to thank all libraries that participate in the interlibrary-loan system. Finally, I am grateful to the park rangers and staff at New Echota State Park in Georgia for use of their library facilities.

CHEROKEE VOICES

Early Accounts of
Cherokee Life in the East

❧·❧

HANDS AND HEARTS JOINED TOGETHER, 1730

❖⯈❖⯈❖⯈❖⯈❖⯈❖⯈❖⯈❖⯈❖⯈❖⯈❖⯈❖⯈❖⯈❖

When Alexander Cuming arrived in South Carolina from Great Britain in December 1729, no formal relationships existed between the Cherokees and the crowns of Europe. The French had established forts and trade posts on the boundaries of the Cherokees' territory but had failed to gain their permanent loyalty. Spanish Florida had supplied the Cherokees with guns for many years but had angered them by capturing ten of their men and killing ten others while they were on a trade mission. The British colony of South Carolina had managed to establish a trade relationship with the Cherokees and had gained a small land cession, but it couldn't count on the Cherokees to support its war against the French in North America.[1]

It took a charismatic but unlikely character, Alexander Cuming, to make the diplomatic breakthrough for Great Britain. Cuming, a Scottish nobleman whose family fortune was depleted, went to Charleston to seek his fortune. He began borrowing money extensively with promissory notes. He bought silver and gold to ship abroad while claiming to establish a new silver standard for the South Carolina economy.[2]

Exactly what possessed Cuming to undertake his expedition deep into Cherokee country is unclear. He probably had several motives. Since he was a member of the Royal Society, one of his goals may have been scientific study. He may have been escaping into the mountains to elude creditors. Or he may have been seeking to establish a name for himself. Whatever the reason, he did not have the authority to make agreements with the Cherokees on behalf of England, but that is exactly what he did, using bribes and his flair for showmanship.[3]

The Cherokee villages were organized into three main town groups—the Overhill Towns along the Little Tennessee River in East Tennessee; the Middle Towns in the mountains of western North Carolina and northeastern Georgia; and the Lower Towns clustered in western South Carolina. Cuming made his way first to Keowee, the powerful seat of the Lower Towns, and then to the Middle Towns. Along the way, he charmed the Cherokees and traders, presenting himself as a representative of His Majesty King George and demanding that they join him in kneeling in loyalty to the king.[4]

When Cuming learned of the existence of an official Cherokee crown, the Crown of Tannassy, he set off for the Overhill

Towns to search for it. He was obsessed with the idea of obtaining the crown, which turned out to be a cap made of possum that was dyed red or yellow. It was Cuming's plan to lay the crown at King George's feet.[5]

The year before Cuming visited the Cherokees, one of their most prominent leaders, Wrosetasatow, had died, leaving a vacancy in leadership. Moytoy, whose name means Rainmaker or Water Conjuror, wanted the position of principal leader of the Cherokees. In exchange for Cuming's support, Moytoy aided him in his quest for the Crown of Tannassy.[6]

In April 1730, at a meeting at Nikwasi, also known as Nikossen and Nequisee, Cuming declared Moytoy emperor of all the Cherokees. The Cherokees then lifted Cuming onto Moytoy's seat and performed the Eagle Tail Dance for him. This involved stroking Cuming with the tail feathers of thirteen golden eagles. Cuming then demanded those present give up the crown, the eagle tails, and the scalps of their enemies to show their submission to King George and to himself.[7]

Having obtained the allegiance of the Cherokees to the British Crown, Cuming returned to England with seven Cherokees, including the young Attakullalkulla, also called Oucounacou or Little Carpenter. Moytoy refused to go to England. Cuming presented the Cherokees, the crown, the eagle tails, and the scalps to King George on June 22, 1730.[8]

A formal treaty declaring the Cherokees loyal subjects of King George was drawn up in September while the Cherokees were still in London. Cuming petitioned to be made the king's official ambassador to, or overlord of, the Cherokees, a position that was denied him. Although he failed to gain that title, he succeeded in encouraging trade between the Cherokees and the British and averting a Cherokee-French alliance.[9]

When Cuming was thrown in debtor's prison in England in 1736, he appealed to King George on the grounds that his father had once saved the king's life. Cuming was eventually released from prison and served as a captain in Jamaica. He wrote his memoirs in 1764 and died in 1775.[10]

Meanwhile, back in America, Moytoy was killed in battle in 1741. The British appointed his thirteen-year-old son, Ammonscossittee, to succeed his father as emperor of the Cherokees. Ammonscossittee's situation was tenuous from the beginning because the Cherokees were a loose federation of town groups that traditionally did not have a single principal chief to whom all the other chiefs reported. Cherokee leaders did not automatically inherit their titles but rather had to earn them. After a rumor spread that Ammonscosittee wanted to sell Cherokee lands to the colony of Virginia, Chota's chief, Old Hop, or Connecorte, took the title of emperor from Ammonscosittee.[11]

Below are three excerpts from records of the Cherokees' visit to London and Cuming's visit with the Cherokees. The first is drawn from the 1730 treaty of trade and loyalty concluded in London. The second is the Cherokees' formal response to that agreement. The third is an excerpt from the memoirs of Alexander Cuming covering his time among the Cherokees. Cuming writes of himself in the third person.

Excerpt from the Articles of Friendship &
Commerce, prepared by the Lord
Commissioners for Trade and Plantations
to the Deputies of the Cherokee Nation in
South Carolina by His Majesty's Order, on
Monday the 7th Day of September 1730

Whereas You Scayagusta Oukah, Chief of the Town of
Tassetsa; —You Scali Cosken, Ketagusta; —You Tethtone; —
You Clogoillah; —You Colannah; —You Oucounacou; —have
been deputed by Moytoy of Telliko, with the Consent and approbation of the whole Nation of the Cherokee Indians, at a
general Meeting at Nikossen the 3d of April 1730, to attend
Sr. Alexander Cuming, Bart. [Baronet] to Great Britain where
you have seen the Great King George at whose Feet the said
Sr. Alexander Cuming, by express Authority for that Purpose
from the said Moytoy and all the Cherokee People has laid
the Crown of your Nation with the Scalps of your Enemies
and Feathers of Glory, at His Majesty's Feet, in Token of your
Obedience.

Now the King of Great Britain, bearing love in His Heart
to the powerfull and great Nation of the Cherokee Indians.
The good Children and Subjects, His Majesty has impowered
us to treat with you here and accordingly we now speak to
you as if the whole Nation of Cherokees, their Old Men, Young
Men, Wives and Children were all present; And you are to
understand the Words we speak as the Words of the Great
King our Master, whom you have seen; And we shall understand the Words which you speak to us as the Words of all

your People with open and true Hearts to the Great King; And thereupon we give—Four Pieces of striped Duffles [coarse woolen fabric often used to make coats].

Hear then the Words of the Great King whom you have seen, and who has commanded us to tell you, That the English every where on all Sides of the great Mountains and Lakes are His People and His Children, whom He loves; That their Friends are His Friends and their Enemies are His Enemies; That he takes it kindly that the great Nation of Cherokees have sent you hither a great way to brighten the chain of Friendship between Him and them; and between your People and His People; that the Chain of Friendship between Him and the Cherokee Indians, is like the Sun, which both Shines here and also upon the great Mountains where they live & equally Warms the Hearts of the Indians and the English; That as there are no Spots or Blackness in the Sun, so is there not any Rust or Foulness in this Chain; And as the Great King has fastned one end of it to His own Breast, He desires you will carry the other end of the Chain, and fasten it well to the Breast of Moytoy of Telliko, and to the Breasts of your old wise Men, your Capts. And all your People, never more to be broken or made loose; And hereupon we give—Two Pieces of Blue Cloth.

The Great King and the Cherokee Indians being thus fastned together by the Chain of Friendship, He has ordered His People and Children the English in Carolina, to trade with the Indians, and to furnish them with all manner of Goods that they want and to make haste to build Houses, and to plant Corn, from Charles Town towards the Town of the

Cherokees, behind the great Mountains, for He desires that the Indians and the English may live together as the Children of one Family, whereas the Great King is a kind and loving Father; And as the King has given His Land on both Sides of the great Mountains to His own Children the English, so He now gives to the Cherokee Indians the Priviledge of living where they please. And hereupon we give—One Piece of Red Cloth.

The great Nation of the Cherokees being now the Children of the Great King of Great Britain, and He their Father, the Cherokees must treat the English as Brethren of the same Family, and must be always ready, at the Governor's command, to fight against any Nation, whether they be White Men or Indians who shall dare to molest or hurt the English; And hereupon we give—Twenty Guns.

The Nation of Cherokees shall on their Part take Care to keep the trading Path clean, and that there be no Blood in the Path where the English white Men tread, even tho' they should be accompanyd by any other People with whom the Cherokees are at War; Whereupon we give—Four Hundred Pounds Weight of Gunpowder.

That the Cherokees shall not suffer their People to trade with the White Men of any other Nation but the English, nor permit White Men of any other Nation to build any Forts, Cabins, or plant Corn amongst them or near to any of the Indian Towns, or upon the Lands w'ch belong to the Great King; and if any such Attempt shall be made, you must acquaint the English Governor therewith and do whatever he directs in order to maintain and defend the Great King's Right to the Country of Carolina; Whereupon we give—Five Hundred Pounds Weight of Swan Shott [large lead pellets] and Five Hundred Pounds Weight of Bullets.

That if any Negroe Slaves shall run away into the Woods from their English Masters, the Cherokee Indians shall endeavour to apprehend them and either bring them back to the Plantation from whence they run away, or to the Governor, and for every Negroe so apprehended and brought back the Indian who brings him shall receive a Gun and a Match Coat, Whereupon we give—A Box of Vermillion, Ten Thousand Gun Flints, and Six Dozen Hatchets.

That if by any accidental Misfortune it should happen, that an English Man should kill an Indian the King or Great Man of the Cherokees shall first complain to the English Governor, and the Man who did it, shall be punished by the English Laws as if he had killed an English Man, and in like manner if an Indian kills an English Man, the Indian who did it, shall be delivered up to the Governor and be punished by the same English Law, as if he was an English Man; Whereupon we give—Twelve Dozen of Spring Knives, Four Dozen of Brass Kettles and Ten Dozen of Belts.

You are to understand all that we have now said, to be the Words of the Great King, whom you have seen and as a Token that His heart is open and true to His Children and Subjects the Cherokees and to all their People, He gives His hand in this Belt, which He desires may be kept and shewn to all your People and to their Children, and Childrens Children to confirm what is now spoken and to bind this Agreement of Peace of Friendship betwixt the English and the

Cherokees, as long as the Mountains and Rivers shall last, or the Sun Shine; Whereupon we give—This Belt of Wampum [strings or sashes of shell beads used for money or in a ceremonial pledge].[12]

Answer of the Indian Chiefs of the Cherokee Nation, the 9th day of September, 1730, to the Propositions made to them, in behalf of His Majesty, by the Board of Trade, on the 7th day of the Same Month

We are come hither from a dark Mountainous Place, where nothing but darkness is to be found; but are now in a place where there is light. There was a person [Alexander Cuming] in our Country with Us, he gave Us a Yellow token of Warlike Honour, that is left with Moytoy of Telliko; and as Warriors, we received it; He came to Us like a Warrior from you, A Man he was, his talk was upright, and the token he left, preserves his Memory amongst Us.

We look upon you as if the Great King George was present; And We love you, as representing the Great King, and shall Dye in the same way of thinking.

The Crown of Our Nation is different from that which the Great King George wears, and from that which We saw in the Tower; But to Us it is all one, and the Chain of Friendship shall be carried to Our People.

We look upon the Great King George as the Sun, and as

Our Father; and upon Ourselves as his Children; For tho' We are red, and you white, yet Our Hands and Hearts are join'd together.

When We shall have acquainted Our People with what We have seen, Our Children from Generation to Generation will always remember it.

In War We shall always be as one with you; The Great King George's Enemies Shall be Our Enemies; His People and Ours shall be always one, and dye together.

We came hither naked and poor, as the Worm out of the Earth, but you have everything, and We that have nothing must love you, and can never break the Chains of Friendship that is between Us.

Here stands the Governor of Carolina, whom We know: This small Rope which We shew you, is all We have to bind our slaves with, and may be broken; but you have Iron Chains for yours, However if we catch your slaves, We shall bind them as well as We can, and deliver them to Our friends again, and have no pay for it.

We have looked round for the Person that was in Our Country, he is not here, however We must say that he talked uprightly to Us, and We shall never forget him.

Your white People may very safely build Houses near Us, We shall hurt nothing that belongs to them, for We are the Children of one Father the Great King, and shall live and Dye together.

. . . This is our way of Talking, which is the same to Us, as your letters in the Book, are to you; And to you, beloved Men, We deliver these Feathers, in confirmation of all We have said, and of Our Agreement to your Articles.[13]

Excerpt from Memoirs of the Life of Sir Alexander Cuming of Culter, Baronet *(1764)*

In the month of September 1729 Sir Alexander Cuming took his departure for South Carolina [and] arrived at Charles Town the first week of December. . . .

On the 13th day of March 1730 Old Stile [Julian calendar], Sir Alexander set out from one of the setlements in South Carolina in order to proceed to the Cherokee Mountains where he was received as their Lawgiver by their Emperor Moytoy of Teliquo, was saluted by his order with 13 Eagles Tails, had the Crown of their Nation & scalps of their Enemics given him.

That upon the 18th day of June 1730 Sir Alexander had the Honour of being introduced to His Majesty King George the Second with Seven Cherokee Warriors by His Majesty's express directions in St. George's Chapel at Windsor when the late Earl of Burlington was installed, when the present Earl of Chesterfield was installed, when His Royal Highness the Duke of Cumberland was installed, and when the Heir apparent to the Crown Fredcrick then Prince of Wales first took his seat as one of the Knights of the Garter, the Savagc Chiefs that dwelt in the Wilderness bowed down before His

Majesty on that occasion as Subjects to the Crown of Great Britain and as a remarkable Token of the Almighty Favour.

On the 22d day of June 1730 Sir Alexander Cuming had an Audience of His Majesty in Windsor Castle being attended by the seven Cherokee Warriors which he had brought over to England as witnesses of the Power conferred upon him on the 3d day of April 1730 O.S. [Old Style] at a place called Nequisee in the Cherokee Mountains and in virtue of the unlimited Power given him by the Cherokee Nation as their Lawgiver Sir Alexander laid the Crown of the Cherokee Nation at His Majestys feet as a token of their Homage and Submission [to] His Majesty as Subjects to the Crown of Great Britain, their Eagles Tails at His Majestys feet as Emblems of Glory and Victory, and four Scalps of their Indian Enemies at His Majestys feet to shew that in their state of savage Liberty they were an over match for any one nation of their indian Enemies and under the conduct of a proper Leader might probably be an over match for many more.[14]

THE PRICE OF A WHITE SHIRT, 1751 – 53

꧂꧂꧂꧂꧂꧂꧂꧂꧂꧂꧂꧂꧂꧂꧂꧂꧂

During the mid-eighteenth century, trade between the British and the Cherokees was at its peak. The British commissioned several traders in the Creek and Cherokee Nations to trade rifles, woolens, tools, and other European goods for skins.

The Cherokees became dependent on trade with the British in the Carolina colony. Skiagunsta, the headman of the Lower Towns, explained, "I am an old man, and have been a warrior, and am a warrior still, and have always told my people to be well with the English for they cannot expect any supply from any where else, nor can they live independent of the English. What are we red people? The clothes we wear, we cannot make ourselves, they are made to us. We use their ammunition with which we kill deer. We cannot make our guns, they are made to us. Every necessary thing in life we must have from the white people."[1]

The trade relationship was not entirely satisfactory to the British either. The first excerpt below is taken from a letter written by an unknown "distressed trader," who seeks to inform Governor James Glen of the state of affairs. The bulk of the excerpt is a price list, which gives a perspective on the value of goods in 1751.

The British, French, and Spanish engaged in intrigue behind the scenes as they manipulated the Indian tribes, including the Cherokees, Creeks, Chickasaws, Choctaws, and Shawnees, to further their interests in the New World. The leaders of the various Cherokee settlements were also vying for power within the Cherokee country. This was a complex time of shifting alliances. Contrary to Alexander Cuming's vision twenty years earlier, the Cherokees recognized no central emperor. Their views on relations with the British and on alliances with the three European powers were not unified.

In July 1753, Governor Glen tried to bring the Cherokees and Creeks together in Charleston to negotiate a peace. The second excerpt below is a portion of that "talk." It is an interchange among Governor Glen and three Cherokees—Skiagunsta of the beleaguered Lower Towns; Overhill leader Long Jack, the headman of the village of Tanase; and Little Carpenter, or Attakullakulla, from Tomotley, one of the Cherokees' most skillful negotiators, and after Old Hop the most important Overhill leader at the time. Skiagunsta is anxious for the peace talk, but the Overhill leaders see a meeting with the Creeks as a distraction from their objective of resolving their trade problems. In fact, the Overhill leaders intentionally delayed their trip to

Charleston until after the Creeks left.[2]

The discussion among Glen and the three Cherokee leaders begins with trade but quickly proceeds to other issues. The Overhill Cherokees promise to make peace with the Creeks if the British will build a fort to protect them and reign in the traders they feel aren't giving them fair prices. The political maneuverings of Little Carpenter and Skiagunsta during this meeting resulted in the construction of Fort Prince George in South Carolina.

Central to the excerpt is a discussion of the fate of some Savannah Indians then being held in Charleston by the British because of acts committed against whites. The Savannahs are probably Shawnee Indians from the Ohio River Valley, with whom Little Carpenter has established peace and trade relations.[3] The Cherokee leaders want them freed. Governor Glen is suspicious of their motives, having received reports that Little Carpenter has been talking with the French and also with the British in Virginia. At the end, Little Carpenter hints at the possibility of uprisings against the British if the Savannahs are not released.

"List of the Prices of Goods"

Nov. 1st, 1751
To his Excellency James Glen, Esq., & honble
Council of So. Carolina

We send this Greeting. We poor Distressed Traders, as

your Honable Council & Assembly has at Present thought proper to bring this Cherokee Trade on a Footing Wherewith will endow us to pay our Creditors which know at Present we are Sufferers.

Imprimis. The Prices of Goods if now Regulated properly as your Excellency and Council both Specifyed no Stillyards [a metal rod with a counterbalance, used for measuring weight] but Scales & Weights to have 1 lb. & 2 lb. Wt. the 1 lb. to be a Deer Skin & 2 lb. To pass a Buck Ditto and if a Skin Weigh more then 2 pounds to Pass for no more than one Skin.

A Blanket	3 Bucks or 6 Does
2 Yards Strouds [coarse wool trade cloth]	3 Bucks or 6 Does
A Garlix [type of imported linen] Shirt	2 Ditto Or 4 Does
Paint, 1 Ounce	1 Doe Skin
Osnbrigs, [coarse linen], 1 Yard	1 Ditto
A Knife	1 Ditto
A large Ditto, Buckhandled	1 Buck
1 Pr. Of Hose	1 Buck and one Doe, or 3 Does &c
Brass Kettles	1 Buck per, or 2 Does
Powder, ¾	1 Doe
60 Bullets	Ditto
Silver Earbobs	1 Buck the Pair
Pea Buttons, per Dozen	1 Doe
Swan Shott [large lead pellets]	200 per a Buck Skin
A Steel [for striking sparks]	1 Doe
A burning Glass	Ditto
Hankerchiefs of India	2 Bucks

Ditto, common	Ditto
1 Riding Sadel	8 Bucks or 16 Does
2 Yards stript Flannen [flannel]	2 Bucks or 4 Does
Fine Rufel Shirts	4 Bucks or 8 Does
Women's Side Sadol	20 Bucks or 40 Does
Men's Shoes	2 Bucks or 4 Does
Callicoes	2 Bucks or 4 Does
Callicoes	Ditto, 1 Buck and 1 Doe, or 3 Does
Fine Ribands [ribbons]	1 Buck 2 Yards, or 4 Does
Gartring [material for making garters]	2 Bucks per piece or 4 Does
Caddice [worsted yarn] Ditto	2 Bucks or 4 Does per piece
2 Yards stompt Flanen	2 Bucks or 4 Does
Worsted Caps	1 Buck and 1 Doe or 3 Does
1 Gun	7 Bucks or 14 Does[4]

Excerpt from Governor Glen's talks with Little Carpenter, Skiagunsta, and others on July 5, 1753, in Charleston

SKIAGUNSTA. I am listening to hear if any of the upper towns has any thing more to say, and have been listening to these two headmen. Suppose they have not done, when they have, I have something to say, for it is not our custom like the white people to talk altogether, but when one is done another begins. When they are all quiet, I shall begin to speak.

GOVERNOR. It is a very good way, and indeed we observe the same.

LONG JACK. We were talking about the trade. I believe both your Excellency and we are imposed on by some traders. When we tell them of it, they say they have the governor's orders for it, and when we complain, we are ill treated by them. The price of a white shirt is at 5 lb. of leather, a hoe at 5 lb., a small shirt at 3 lb. If we complain of this, they answer they have come a great way, and that their horses brake their bones in coming over the hills. Some of them make us pay 6 lb. of leather for a fathom of calico and 4 lbs. weight for one yard.

GOVERNOR. What the traders say is very true. They often sustain great losses in bringing in their goods to your nation, and often have them spoiled in the carriage, and indeed the price is so low that many of them cannot live. Sometimes they cannot be paid for the goods that they do sell, and many other disadvantages there are that they labour under, so that you must not expect to have goods at too low a price, for by the last treaty, you were to have goods at the same price, as was usual before the making [of] that treaty.

LONG JACK. Many of us are often killed in the war, and others by sickness, and if we do owe the traders any thing they must not seize upon our horses, for the debt, though it be little, when what is left would be of service to the living.

GOVERNOR. I am very sorry to hear it. If you will mention but any one of the traders that do such things, they shall be punished. But you yourselves ought to keep accompts to compare with their accompts. These are the words in the last treaty. . . .

It was stipulated that goods should stand at the usual prices, and that if any trader should impose on them they should be punished. Let me know the person that does it.

LITTLE CARPENTER. A flap [broad piece of material] to be one pound of leather, and 6 flaps to be the measure of a match coat.

GOVERNOR. A match coat is settled at 6 wt. of Leather. The Creeks pay 8 wt., and that weight is really 10. (To the interpreter) Tell them they may have an iron yard up with them, and the trader cannot cheat them.

SKIAGUNSTA. When I and my people were here before now, we agreed as to the price of goods, a flap, a shirt, &c., but before it was settled, something intervened that stopped it.

LITTLE CARPENTER. It was on account of the trade that we went to Virginia. When I was in England I was told that I might go any way for goods when I could get them the cheapest. The price of shirting is dearer now than formerly.

GOVERNOR. It was agreed that the price should be as had been usual.

LITTLE CARPENTER. The traders are very cross with us Indians. We dare not speak to them. If we do, they take our skins, and throw them on the ground, and deny us goods. If we do not give them their prices we must go without any.

GOVERNOR. You have already got measures and weights, and therefore they cannot cheat you, and the prices of goods are so very low that the traders cannot live, and pay for their goods, but I desire you will tell me any one that ever got a farthing among you. One of the greatest traders who used to supply the others in your country with goods, because our traders among you were not able to pay for the goods, they bought of him, is gone off to another country and broke. There is James Beamer here who went very young into your country to settle as a trader. He is now grey headed and yet in debt, and indeed the traders among the Creeks make but a Shift [a small share or portion] to live. This is all they can do, and even Mr. Kelly who was a long time among you, he left nothing, for his wife and children are poor. . . .

LITTLE CARPENTER. Do what we can, the white people will cheat us in our weights and measures, and make them less. What is it a trader can not do? They cheat us in the measure of our powder. Some of the white men borrowed my yeard [yard] and cut it, and then gave it back for which I was blamed.

GOVERNOR. Let the Yeard measure be kept by one of your beloved men, and if then any trader cut it, send to me.

LITTLE CARPENTER. We are satisfied.

LONG JACK. I want to know what is to be done with the prisoners below.

GOVERNOR. Does he know what nation they are of?

LONG JACK. Yes. They are Savannahs.

GOVERNOR. Was you ever in their country?

LONG JACK. Yes.

GOVERNOR. How did they behave when you was last in their Country?

LONG JACK. They behaved very kindly to the white people.

GOVERNOR. Did you not hear that they killed a white man in their country?

LONG JACK. Yes, but he was killed by a party of French Indians.

GOVERNOR. I was informed that one of your nation was in the Savanah Town at that Time, and saw the Savannah stick a Knife in the white Man's Belly. Did you never hear of that?

LONG JACK. Yes, I did, but it was not a Savannah, but one of the Five Nations who was very much in debt to this trader. They got drunk together, quarreled, and he killed the white man.

GOVERNOR. Did you see it?

LONG JACK. I heard of it.

GOVERNOR. (To the interpreter) Ask if he has not heard that they have killed several white men since that time? Did you not hear of it in your nation?

LONG JACK. Yes.

GOVERNOR. Were such people to be looked upon as friends?

LONG JACK. These seven men were Savanah traders, who in returning home were killed by French Indians.

GOVERNOR. (To the interpreter) Ask if ever he heard of two Savannah fellows going into the house of a white man in our settlements, were hospitably received, and the master of the house spoke the Savanah language, and gave them a supper, and kind usage, but who, when the master of the house was in bed and asleep, shot him dead, killed another young man sleeping on the ground, and two poor children, they also murdered in their beds. And wounded the mother in such a manner that they left her for dead, then plundered the house and took every thing away with them. The women recovered a little so much as to be brought here and have her wounds dressed, but died a little time after of those wounds; only before she died she declared that they were Savannah fellows that committed the murder for her husband who was murdered, before his [death] told her so for he spoke the Savanah language.

LONG JACK. I was at Kewee when these two fellows came there, and I sent notice immediately to the Raven [probably the headman of Toxaway] to come and talk with them about it. He reprimanded them bitterly for what they had done, one of them was a Tawaw, the other, a Savanah who had when young been kept prisoner among the Senecas.

GOVERNOR. As to the Savanahs below, when we took them we found strings to bind prisoners with. We asked what the use of these strings was. They owned it was to bind the prisoners they could ketch, of our friendly Indians, a people who make war with nobody. (Pointing to King Jonney, the Notchee Indian) there is one of the said settlement Indians who was taken prisoner by them and carried to Kewee, but made his escape from them.

LITTLE CARPENTER. It was I that tied him the 2d Time he was taken.

GOVERNOR. As a further proof one of our white people saw 14 Indians in a boat with 14 paddles. They went upon an island to the southward, carried off 14 of our settlement Indians and killed two. Are these the actions of friends? But I shall not quarrel with a whole nation for the sake of a few, only shall punish the offenders, though as to that we are not come to any determined resolution, though we can not think them innocent, for they had no business down in our settlements. We have heard a good many things about their nation, and shall keep them till we hear further, but this is an affair that does not concern you. (To the interpreter) Tell them that there is strong presumption of their guilt since they had no business here, but if they had been Cherokees who had done the like, we should have served them in the same manner as we do these Savannah prisoners, but for all that should not have broke with the Cherokee Nation.

LONG JACK. I should not speak in their favour, only we look on them as on our own people, as they always come with peace talks, to our nation, and we desire they may be given to us.

GOVERNOR. I have heard so much of the irregularities of their nation, and that we shall keep them prisoners till we hear further of their behaviour (To the interpreter) Tell them this is no business of theirs.

SKIAGUNSTA. I hope the discourse will be dropped as I have a few words to say.

GOVERNOR. Go on.

SKIAGUNSTA. I look towards the southwest, and it looks bright. I am heartily glad of the peace, and we are obliged to your Excellency for it, and I am ready to confirm it. I have shaken hands with the Creeks, and like the talk, but I should be better satisfied to see them here; we are but two towns at present in the Lower Cherokees, but we are men and warriors as well as the others, and we have a war hatchet as well as they, but as soon as I heard the peace talk, we buried the bloody hatchet under ground, and it never shall appear any more. My heart was glad to hear of peace. I had no opportunity myself to go to the Creeks, but I sent a message by a white man that I was willing and ready to be at peace with them. Some time after, I and one of the Creeks came down and met as friends, the Creek fellow told them that some of the towns were willing to be at peace, but that other towns were not. The man offered to go into the nation with them. But whether they took them for friends or not, some of our people were killed just by our towns. A young man that escaped brought word to our nation that the upper towns were for a peace, but the lower were not. You then sent your agent to propose a peace, and you have obtained it, and I am glad of it for all since that have been quiet. After the agent went to the nation, we lost men last year in the fall, but we did not seek revenge for them, perhaps they were out and did not hear of the peace. Therefore what ever injury was done we resolved to bear it patiently, till we heard your Excellency's talk, and then appeal to you for redress. Last winter one came to Estatoe & told us, that all was peace. That made our hearts glad, and we then hunted without fear. When I went home I told my people that all was peace, and charged them not to spoil it, and that in case a Creek should kill a Cherokee, not to revenge it, but to complain thereof to your Excellency, and to have all differences and disputes between the two nations, to be determined by you, by which means the peace might be lasting.

For myself, I have always been obedient in every shape to the Governor's command and followed him step by step. I have none other now to assist me, but your Excellency, but what follows is the last speech I am going to make. Your Excellency must remember that you promised to build a Fort at Kewee, which has not been done, though I earnestly desire it may be. Otherwise we in the Lower Cherokees will not be able to keep our towns.

GOVERNOR. I have heard what you have said, and the long account how the peace was brought about. I shall always continue my good offices, to preserve it. I hope the peace will be lasting, and then there will be no occasion for a fort. I remember I promised a fort. Whenever I promise, I will always perform it. It is the practice of the English always to perform what they promise, but many things happened, and some bad talks among the Cherokees prevailed, but now every thing seems to be settled. I shall endeavour to have a fort there, though there is not so great occasion as it is peace.

SKIAGUNSTA. I shall be very glad to be dispatched, but I do not know when I shall get home as I have lost my horse. Perhaps some rogue of a white man has taken him.

GOVERNOR. Diligent search shall be made for the horse, and if he cannot be found, you shall have another to carry you home and to keep him.

LONG JACK. I shall be glad to know what is to be done with the six Savanahs? For the old man at home will be very anxious to know what will become of them. They always have behaved like messengers of peace.

GOVERNOR. (To the interpreter) Tell them that these Savannahs have not behaved so well as they ought, we have not resolved as yet what to do with them.

LONG JACK. They come to us with talks of peace.

GOVERNOR. (To the interpreter) Tell them they may have business at Chote by bringing talks of peace there, but they have no business at all here in our settlements. It will take a pretty long time to deliberate on what we shall do with them.

LONG JACK. If they brought strings to tie prisoners it was not for white but red people. If they had a mind to kill white people they might have done it before they came here.

GOVERNOR. It is for that reason for seizing red people that we punish them. If any Indian come into our settlements, and tell us they will not hurt white people, for all that, if they should kill the Creeks or Cherokees whom they might find in our settlements, we should punish them for it, though at the same time we should not differ with the nation to whom they belong.

LONG JACK. If you will not take our talks about the Indians, we will not take your talk about a peace with the Creeks and us.

GOVERNOR. You have no business with our affairs.

LITTLE CARPENTER. We will not make peace with Creeks whilst these prisoners are here.

GOVERNOR. I am sorry to repeat my words again. It is the last time I shall do so. (To the interpreter) Tell him if any Cherokee had done the same we would punish him, and yet remain friends with the Cherokee Nation. We never suffer Indians to meddle in our affairs. You say you came from Old Hop [Chota's chief], but that you would say nothing yourselves till you heard and should tell him all that I did say. Therefore I do not mind what you say about the Savanahs.

LITTLE CARPENTER. It's true Old Hop sent us with a talk, but what shall we say were we to go home and not bring him a talk about those Indians? The old man would be very cross and will not listen to any peace with the Creeks. I do not vindicate the Savanahs, but it is for the sake of the white people that come among us, for if these Indians are punished the path will be made bloody, and no white man be able to come to us. As for you, and those about you (pointing to the governor) you are safe, but many straggling white man will lose their Lives.

GOVERNOR. What Indian dare do so?

LITTLE CARPENTER. There are many of the 5 Nations will join these people, and some of the Cherokees also will do the same, which we cannot prevent. It is true the Savannahs are not of the 5 Nations, but the Five Nations will join them.

GOVERNOR. The Savanahs never go into the councils of the Five Nations, but if the Savanahs did so themselves, we would soon rout them out.

LITTLE CARPENTER. There are three towns of them.

GOVERNOR. If they were thirty we have men enough to destroy them all.

LITTLE CARPENTER. It is not for the quantity. We know you may cut them off, but in the mean time they may do a great deal of mischief.

GOVERNOR. We are not affrayed of the French Indians. We are determined to defend our friendly Indians. Old Hop says he has sent down his boys, and I am sorry to find they behave like boys. If these people are guilty we shall punish them. If not, they will be acquitted. It is not for our own sakes that we desire peace. It is at your own earnest desire for which I have been pressed and solicited by your own nation by letters from the lower and middle settlements, and the other towns, but if you covet war rather than peace, you shall have it, and I shall write to the Creeks about it, that you may have enough of war. Finis.[5]

A Second Peace, 1761 – 62

❧❦❧❦❧❦❧❦❧❦❧❦❧❦❧❦❧❦❧❦❧❦❧❦❧❦

In February 1760, twenty-three Cherokee leaders were murdered by the British at Fort Prince George in South Carolina. In response, Ostenaco, also known as Tassitte, Judd's Friend, or Skyacust Ukah (see portrait on front cover), led a siege at Fort Loudon, cutting off its provisions and causing its surrender several months later. As Captain Paul Demeré led his men out of the fort, Ostenaco and other Cherokees attacked and killed twenty-three of the British soldiers in retaliation for the Cherokee deaths at Fort Prince George. Shortly after this incident, Ostenaco was among those who called for peace with the English. However, the British sent an army against the Middle Settlements, during which they burned villages and fields. In September 1761, Attakullakulla negotiated a peace between the British and the Cherokees.[1]

It was against this background of betrayal, murder, and

strained relations between Carolina settlers and the Cherokees that the Virginians decided to establish a fort in Cherokee country. An army of Virginia militia constructed a fort on the Long Island of the Holston River, also called the Great Island, at what is now Kingsport, Tennessee. It was named Fort Robinson. A delegation of Cherokees visiting Fort Robinson requested that an ambassador be sent to the Overhill Towns to explain the new treaty between the Cherokees and the Virginia colony. Henry Timberlake, a junior officer, volunteered for the mission.[2]

Timberlake set out in late November 1761 in a dugout canoe. One of the men with him was John McCormack, who had lived in the Cherokee country for many years. McCormack would serve as an interpreter. When they arrived in the Overhill Towns, Ostenaco greeted them warmly. Timberlake lived with the Cherokees several months as Ostenaco's personal guest. It is believed that he fathered a child, Richard Timberlake, by one of Ostenaco's daughters during his stay with the Cherokees.[3]

When Timberlake finally returned to Williamsburg, Virginia, a large Cherokee delegation, including Ostenaco, accompanied him. Ostenaco met the governor and requested an introduction to King George III. Arrangements were made for Ostenaco, Timberlake, and others to sail to England to meet the king.[4] When they were finally granted an audience, the meeting was rather awkward, due to Timberlake's difficulties in interpreting the Cherokee language.[5] Upon his return to Charleston on November 3, 1762, Ostenaco gave a triumphant speech to the colonial council describing his trip to see the king.[6]

Years later, Attakullakulla and other Cherokee leaders signed away many Cherokee lands to a speculator, Richard Henderson, during a treaty meeting at Sycamore Shoals. Ostenaco took no part in the treaty. Dragging Canoe, nephew of Attakullakulla, became upset over his uncle's forfeiture of Cherokee lands and withdrew from the Overhill Towns. He, Ostenaco, and many other Cherokees moved south and established the Lower Towns. These towns became home to a group of disaffected Cherokees, Creeks, Tories, and runaway slaves who became known as the Chickamaugans. Ostenaco died of old age at his home on Judd's Creek in Chickamauga territory sometime around 1780.[7]

Below are a pair of excerpts from Timberlake's memoirs detailing his time among the Cherokees in 1761 and 1762.

The first is an account of his arrival. Timberlake listens to a speech of peace given by Ostenaco. Afterward, upon being treated to some Cherokee hospitality, he reveals his difficulties in adjusting to a new culture. The footnotes are Timberlake's own.

The second excerpt includes speeches by Ostenaco and another Cherokee chief. It gives an overview of the shifting loyalties and the conflicts among Indian groups in the early 1760s. When news arrives of Cherokee deaths at the hands of northern Indians believed to be allied with the British, Timberlake fears for his own safety; the Cherokees, however, display restraint. Later, a party led by Willinawaw reaches the village after a Cherokee attack on northern Indians. The excerpt also makes reference to some white prisoners held as slaves by the Cherokees who captured them. Ostenaco apparently consents to free them to Fort Prince George, though further complications delay the transfer.

Excerpts from
The Memoirs of Lieut. Henry Timberlake

EXCERPT 1

Within four or five miles of the nation, the Slave Catcher [an old Cherokee with whose party of ten or twelve Indians Timberlake traveled for two days] sent his wife forward by land, partly to prepare a dinner, and partly to let me have her place in his canoe, seeing me in pain, and unaccustomed to such hard labour, which seat I kept till about two o'clock, when we arrived at his house, opposite the mouth of Tellequo river, compleating a twenty-two days course of continual fatigues, hardships, and anxieties.

Our entertainment from these people was as good as the country could afford, consisting of roast, boiled, and fried meats of several kinds, and very good Indian bread, baked in a very curious manner. After making a fire on the hearth-stone, about the size of a large dish, they sweep the embers off, laying a loaf smooth on it; this they cover with a sort of deep dish, and renew the fire upon the whole, under which the bread bakes to as great perfection as in any European oven.

We crossed the river next morning, with some Indians that had been visiting in that neighbourhood, and went to Tommotly, taking Fort Loudon in the way, to examine the ruins.

We were received at Tommotly in a very kind manner by Ostenaco, the commander in chief, who told me, he had already given me up for lost, as the gang I parted with at the

Great Island had returned about ten days before, and that my servant was then actually preparing for his return, with news of my death.

After smoaking and talking some time, I delivered a letter from Colonel Stephen, and another from Captain M'Neil, with some presents from each, which were gratefully accepted by Ostenaco and his consort. He gave me a general invitation to his house, while I resided in the country; and my companions found no difficulty in getting the same entertainment, among an hospitable, tho' savage people, who always pay a great regard to any one taken notice of by their chiefs.

Some days after, the headmen of each town were assembled in the town-house of Chote, the metropolis of the country, to hear the articles of peace read, whither the interpreter and I accompanied Ostenaco.

The town-house, in which are transacted all public business and diversions, is raised with wood, and covered over with earth, and has all the appearance of a small mountain at a little distance. It is built in the form of a sugar loaf, and large enough to contain 500 persons, but extremely dark, having, besides the door, which is so narrow that but one at a time can pass, and that after much winding and turning, but one small aperture to let the smoak out, which is so ill contrived, that most of it settles in the roof of the house. Within it has the appearance of an ancient amphitheatre, the seats being raised one above another, leaving an area in the middle, in the center of which stands the fire; the seats of the head warriors are nearest it.

They all seemed highly satisfied with the articles. The

peace-pipe was smoaked, and Ostenaco made an harangue to the following effect:

"The bloody tommahawke, so long lifted against our brethren the English, must now be buried deep, deep in the ground, never to be raised again*; and whoever shall act contrary to any of these articles, must expect a punishment equal to his offence†. Should a strict observance of them be neglected, a war must necessarily follow, and a second peace may not be so easily obtained. I therefore once more recommend to you, to take particular care of your behaviour towards the English, whom we must now look upon as ourselves; they have the French and Spaniards to fight, and we enough of our own colour, without medling with either nation. I desire likewise, that the white warrior, who has ventured himself here with us, may be well used and respected by all, wherever he goes amongst us."

The harrange being finished, several pipes were presented me by the headsmen, to take a whiff. This ceremony I could have waved, as smoaking was always very disagreeable to me; but as it was a token of their amity, and they might be offended if I did not comply, I put on the best face I was able, though I dared not even wipe the end of the pipe that came out of their mouths; which, considering their paint and dirtiness, are not of the most *ragoutant* [tasty], as the French term it.

After smoaking, the eatables were produced, consisting chiefly of wild meat; such as venison, bear, and buffalo; tho' I cannot much commend their cookery, every thing being greatly overdone: there were likewise potatoes, pumpkins, homminy, boiled corn, beans, and pease, served up in small flat baskets, made of split canes, which were distributed amongst the croud; and water, which, except the spirituous liquor brought by the Europeans, is their only drink, was handed about in small goards. What contributed greatly to render this feast disgusting, was eating without knives and forks, and being obliged to grope from dish to dish in the dark. After the feast there was a dance; but I was already so fatigued with the ceremonies I had gone through, that I retired to Kanagatucko's hot-house**; but was prevented taking any repose by the smoke, with which I was almost suffocated, and the croud of Indians that came and sat on the bed-side; which indeed was not much calculated for repose to any but Indians, or those that had passed an apprenticeship to their ways, as I had done: it was composed of a few boards, spread with bear-skins, without any other covering; the house being so hot, that I could not endure the weight of my own blanket.

* As in this speech several allusions are made to the customs of the Indians, it may not be impertinent to acquaint the reader, that their way of declaring war, is by smoking a pipe as a bond among themselves, and lifting up a hatchet stained in blood, as a menace to their enemies; at declaring peace this hatchet is buried, and a pipe smoked by both parties, in token of friendship and reconciliation.

† The chiefs can inflict no punishment; but, upon the signing of the peace, it was agreed by both nations, that offend-

ers on either side should be deliverd up to be punished by the offended party, and it is to this the Chief alludes.

** The Hot-House [of Kanagatucko, one of the headmen at Chota] is a little hut joined to the house, in which a fire is continually kept, and the heat so great, that cloaths are not to be borne the coldest day in winter.[8]

EXCERPT 2

On the 26th of January [1762], advices were received from the Great Island, that some Cherokees had been killed by the northern Indians, who had been encouraged, and much caressed, by the commanding officer. This piece of news seemed greatly to displease them; they suspended however their judgment, till further intelligence. I began to be very uneasy for the return of an express [special messenger] I had sent out on my arrival, who was to come back by the Great Island, and was the only person who could give me any accounts I could rely on, as I was sensible the Indian one was infinitely exaggerated. We were yet talking of this, when the *News Hallow* [a special call or yell] was given from the top of Tommotly town-house; whereupon Ostenaco rose from the table, and went immediately to the town-house, where he staid till day. On asking him next morning, What news? he seemed very unwilling to tell me, and went out of the house, seemingly very much displeased. I then made the same question to several other Indians, whole different stories convinced me it was something they endeavoured to conceal.

I was under some apprehension at this unusual incivility. It was no wonder I was alarmed; had the English given any encourgement to these northern ravagers, nay, had the French faction persuaded their countrymen of our countenancing them in the slaughter, the meanest of the deceased's relations had it in his power to sacrifice me to their maues [in-laws], and would certainly have done it, since, in default of kindred, their revenge falls on any of the same country that unfortunately comes within their reach; and nothing could be a protection to an hostage, when capitulating could not save the garrison of Fort Loudoun: a body of Indians pursued them, and breaking through the articles, and all the laws of war and humanity, surprised and butchered them. Disguising, however, my uneasiness, I seemingly took to some diversions, while I sent M'Cormack to pry into the true cause of such a change; he following my host, found no difficulty in shuffling amongst the crowd into the town-house, where Ostenaco made the following speech.

"We have had some talks lately from the Great Island, which I hope nevertheless are not true, as I should be very sorry that the peace, so lately concluded with our brethren the English, should be broke in so short a time: we must not judge as yet of what we have heard from the Great Island. If Bench the express [a Cherokee messenger] does not return soon, I myself will raise a party and go to the Great Island, where I shall get certain information of all that has happened."

This speech was received with shouts of applause, and the assembly betook themselves to dancing.

On the 28th, I was invited to a grand eagle's tail dance, at which about 600 persons of both sexes were assembled. About midnight, in the heat of their diversion, news was brought of the death of one of their principal men, killed at the Great Island by the northern Indians. This put a sudden stop to their diversion, and nothing was heard but threats of vengeance. I easily concluded that this could only proceed from the confirmation of the ill news already received. I tried as much as laid in my power to mollify their anger by telling them, that, if any accident had happened to their people, it was neither by consent or approbation of the English; that tho' the northern Indians were our allies as well as they, I was certain more favour would be shewn them than their enemies, as Capt. M'Neil, who commanded the fort, was a good, humane, brave officer, and had always shewn so much friendship for their nation, as to leave no room to doubt of his protection to any of their people who should be under his care. This satisfied them so well, that some proposed dancing again; but as it was late, they agreed to give over their diversion for that night.

On the 4th of February, an account came in almost contradictory to this. An Indian woman from Holston's River was the messenger, who related, that the northern Indians had turned their arms against the English, and were then actually building a breast-work within a quarter of a mile of Fort Robinson; that, whilst one half were employed in carrying on the work, the other observed the motions of our people; but this lie was even too gross for Indians to digest; tho' the next day, another who came in confirmed it, and moreover affirmed the enemy's fortifications to be already breast high.

The 15th was the day appointed for the return of the Little Carpenter; and his not arriving began to give his friends a great deal of uneasiness. Ostenaco bore likewise his share in it, as his brother was of the party. Here is a lesson to Europe; two Indian chiefs, whom we call barbarians, rivals of power, heads of two opposite factions, warm in opposing one another, as their interest continually clash; yet these have no farther animosity, no family-quarrels or resentment, and the brother of the chief who had gained the superiority is a volunteer under his rival's command.

For my part, I was no less anxious about the express. I dispatched my servant out to meet him, and bring me the particulars of what had been transacted at the Great Island; he returned in about five or six days, with the letters the express had been charged with, leaving him to make out the rest of the journey as his fatigue would permit. Among others was a letter from Capt. M'Neil, informing me, that a party of about seventy northern Indians came to Fort Robinson a short time after I had left it, who told him, that they came from Pittsburg, with a pass from the commanding officer, to join us against the Cherokees, not knowing that we had already concluded a peace. They seemed very much dissatisfied at coming so far to no purpose, and demanded if any Cherokees were near? They were answered, that a party were out a hunting; but, if they would be looked upon as friends to the English, they must not meddle with them, while under the protection of the commanding officer. The Indians, however, paying but little regard to this admonition, went immediately in pursuit of them, and finding them a few hours after, as in no apprehension of any enemy, they fired on them before they discovered themselves, killing one, and wounding another, who however made his escape to the fort. His countrymen all did the same, without returning the fire, as few of their guns were loaded, and they inferior in number. Their enemies pursued them to the fort, but could never see them after, as Capt. M'Neil took great care to keep them asunder. Finding therefore no more likelihood of scalping, the northern Indians marched away from the fort.

This was the same party I encamped with the first night after my departure from the Great Island, and were surprised at the same place, where they had still continued.

He farther informed me, that I should probably find Fort Robinson, and all the posts on the communication, evacuated, as the regiment was to be broke.

I made this letter public, with which they seemed tolerably well satisfied, particularly when I feigned the wounded Indian was under the care of an English surgeon, who would not fail to cure him in a little time.

I now began to be very desirous of returning, and acquainted Ostenaco of my anxiety, desiring him to appoint fifteen or twenty headmen, agreeable to the orders I had received from Col. Stephen, as likewise to collect all the white persons and negroes, to be sent conformable to the articles of peace, to Fort Prince George. He replied, that, as soon as the white prisoners returned from hunting, where they then were with their masters (the white people becoming slaves, and the property of those that take them) he would set about the performance. Some time after this, when all the prisoners were come in, I again attacked Ostenaco; but then his horses could not be found, and there was a necessity of having one or two to carry my baggage and his own. I then waited till the horses were found; but when I supposed all things ready for our departure, I was greatly surprised to find it delayed. Ostenaco told me, that one of the Carpenter's party, which was on its return home, had come in the night before, and reported, that the Carolinians had renewed the war before they had well concluded a peace. The Indian had, according to custom, a long account of it; but tho' I shewed the improbability of such a story, Ostenaco refused to set out before the Carpenter arrived, which was not till the 23d following. He brought in the same report, but owned he did not believe it, as it was told him by a person who he thought wanted to raise some disturbance.

I now began to be very pressing with Ostenaco, threatening if he would not set out immediately, to return without him. This however would have been my last resource, as I was for the space of 140 miles ignorant of every step of the way. I at last prevailed on him; but on the 10th of March, while we were again preparing for our departure, the *Death Hallow* [a special call or yell] was heard from the top of Tommotly town-house. This was to give notice of the return of a party commanded by Willinawaw, who went to war towards the Shawnese country some time after my arrival. After so many disappointments, I began to think I should never get away, as I supposed this affair would keep me, as others had done, two or three days, and till some new accident should intervene to detain me longer. About eleven o'clock the Indians, about forty in number, appeared within sight of the town; as they approached, I observed four scalps, painted red on the fleshside, hanging on a pole, and carried in front of the line, by the second in command, while Willinawaw brought up the rear. When near the town-house, the whole marched round it three times, singing the war-song and at intervals giving the *Death Hallow*; after which, sticking the pole just by the door, for the crowd to gaze on, they went in to relate in what manner they had gained them. Curiosity prompted me to follow them into the town-house; where, after smoaking a quarter of an hour in silence, the chief gave the following account of their campaign.

"After we left Tommotly, which was about the middle of January, we travelled near 400 miles before we saw the least sign of the enemy; at last, one evening, near the river Ohio, we heard the report of several guns, whereupon I sent out several scouts to discover who they were, and if possible where they encamped, that we might attack them early next morning; about dark the scouts returned, and informed us they were a party of Shawnese, hunting buffaloes; that they had watched them to the river-side, where, taking to their canoes, they had paddled across the river; and seeing a great many fires on the other side, where our scouts directed our fight, we concluded it to be a large encampment; we thereupon began to consult, whether it would be more adviseable to cross the river over night, or early next morning: it was decided in favour of the former, notwithstanding its snowing excessively hard, lest we should be discovered. We accordingly stripped ourselves, tying our guns to our backs, with the buts upwards, to which we hung our ammunition, to prevent its getting wet; we then took water, and swam near half a mile to the other side, where we huddled together to keep ourselves warm, intending to pass the remainder of the night in that manner, and to fall on the enemy at daybreak; but as it continued snowing the whole time, it proved so cold, that we could endure it no longer than a little past midnight, when we resolved to surround the enemy's camp, giving the first fire, and, without charging again, run on them with our tommahawkes, which we had tucked in our belts for that purpose, should there be occasion. We accordingly surrounded them; but when the signal was given for firing; scarce one fourth of our guns went off, wet with the snow, notwithstanding all the precautions we had taken to preserve them dry: we then rushed in; but, before we came to a close engagement, the enemy returned our fire; as, it was at random, not being able to see us before we were upon them, on account of the darkness of the night, and the thickness of the bushes, we received no damage. They had not time to charge again, but sought us with the buts of their guns, tommahawkes, and firebrands. In the beginning of the battle we took two prisoners, who were continually calling out to their countrymen to fight strong, and they would soon conquer us; this made them fight much bolder, till the persons who had the prisoners in custody put a stop to it, by sinking a tommahawke in each of their skulls, on which their countrymen took to flight, and left every thing behind them. As soon as it was day, we examined the field, where we found two more of the enemy dead, one of which was a French warrior, which, with the prisoners we had killed, are the four scalps we have brought in. We lost only one man, the poor brave Raven of Toqua, who ran rashly before us in the midst of the enemy. We took what things we could conveniently bring with us, and destroyed the rest."

Having finished his account of the expedition, out of his shot-pouch he pulled a piece of paper, wrapped up in a bit of birch-bark, which he had taken out of the Frenchman's pocket, and gave it to me to look at, asking if I did not think it was his commission? I replied in the negative, telling him it was only some private marks of his own, which I did not understand. It appears to me to have been his journal.[9]

Welcome in Their Country As
a Friend and Brother, 1776

✦◄✦◄✦◄✦◄✦◄✦◄✦◄✦◄✦◄✦◄✦◄✦◄✦◄✦

In April 1773, William Bartram set sail from Philadelphia to begin a remarkable trip of exploration of the American Southeast. The trip would take nearly five years and would cover four states. During this journey of discovery, Bartram, the son of John Bartram, a fellow of the Royal Society and botanist for the king of Britain, would employ ships, horses, dugout canoes, and trade caravans for transport around the frontier. A trained naturalist, he recorded the flora, fauna, geology, geography, and customs of the indigenous peoples of the region. These notes were published in 1791 in Philadelphia and the following year in London as *Bartram's Travels through North and South Carolina, Georgia, East & West Florida, the Cherokee Country, the Extensive Territories of the Muscogulges, or Creek Confederacy, and the Country of the Chactaws;*

Containing an Account of the Soil and Natural Productions of Those Regions, Together with Observations on the Manners of the Indians.

Bartram was nervous about traveling in Cherokee territory because the Cherokees had been "lately ill-treated by the frontier Virginians; blood being spilt between them, and the injury not yet wiped away by formal treaty: the Cherokees extremely jealous of white people travelling about their mountains, especially if they should be seen peeping in amongst the rocks, or digging up their earth."[1]

In spite of his reservations, Bartram traveled extensively in Cherokee country. He attended a treaty meeting in Augusta, Georgia, between the Creeks and Cherokees, explored the remote forests and peaks of the southern Appalachians, and visited Cherokee villages and trading posts.

After 225 years, Bartram's eyewitness accounts of the Cherokees and other southeastern tribes still provide a wealth of firsthand information of their world during the late eighteenth century.

In the excerpt below, Bartram is traveling into Cherokee territory when he encounters Little Carpenter, who inquires about the welfare of John Stuart, the Indian agent for the Southern colonies. Back in 1760, Little Carpenter had negotiated to save Stuart's life during hostilities around Fort Loudoun in what is now East Tennessee.[2] Following his encounter with Little Carpenter, Bartram rethinks his venture into Cherokee country. On his way out of the territory, he passes through the Cherokee settlement of Cowe—which he describes in some detail, and where he is present during a festival—and the Lower Towns of Keowe and Sinica.

Following the narrative excerpt is Bartram's list of the Cherokee villages that existed at the time of his travels.

Excerpt from William Bartram's
Travels through North & South Carolina, Georgia, East & West Florida . . .

Soon after crossing this large branch of the Tanase, I observed, descending the heights at some distance, a company of Indians, all well mounted on horseback; they came rapidly forward: on their nearer approach I observed a chief at the head of the caravan, and apprehending him to be the Little Carpenter, emperor or grand chief of the Cherokees, as they came up I turned off from the path to make way, in token of respect, which compliment was accepted, and gratefully and magnanimously returned; for his highness with a gracious and cheerful smile came up to me, and clapping his hand on his breast, offered it to me, saying, I am Ata-cul-culla; and heartily shook hands with me, and asked me if I knew it. I answered, that the Good Spirit who goes before me spoke to me, and said, that is the great Ata-cul-culla; and added, that I was of the tribe of white men, of Pennsylvania, who esteem themselves brothers and friends to the red men, but particularly so to the Cherokees, and that notwithstanding we dwelt at so great a distance, we were united in love and friendship, and that the name of Ata-cul-culla was dear to his white brothers of Pennsylvania.

After this compliment, which seemed to be acceptable, he inquired if I came lately from Charleston, and if John Stewart [Stuart] was well, saying that he was going to see him. I replied, that I came lately from Charleston on a friendly visit to the Cherokees; that I had the honour of a personal acquaintance with the superintendant, the beloved man, whom, I saw well but the day before I set off, and who, by letters to the principal white men in the nation, recommended me to the friendship and protection of the Cherokees. To which the great chief was pleased to answer very respectfully, that I was welcome in their country as a friend and brother; and then shaking hands heartily bid me farewell, and his retinue confirmed it by an united voice of assent. After giving my name to the chief, requesting my compliments to the superintendant, the emperor moved, continuing his journey for Charleston; and I, yet persisting in my intention of visiting the Overhill towns, continued on. Leaving the great forest I mounted the high hills, descending them again on the other side, and so on repeatedly for several miles, without observing any variation in the natural productions since passing the Jore: and perceiving the slow progress of vegetation in this mountainous, high country; and, upon serious consideration, it appearing very plainly that I could not, with entire safety, range the Overhill settlements until the treaty was over, which would not come on till late in June; I suddenly came to a resolution to defer these researches at this time, and leave them for the employment of another season and more favourable opportunity, and return to Dartmouth in Georgia, to be ready to join a company of adventurers who were to set off in July for Mobile in West Florida. The leader of this company had been recommended to me as a fit person to assist me on so long and hazardous a journey, through the vast territories of the Creeks.

Therefore next day I turned about on my return, proceeding moderately, being engaged in noting such objects as appeared to be of any moment, and collecting specimens; and in the evening of next day arrived again at Cowe.

Next morning Mr. Galahan [the head trader at Cowe] conducted me to the chief of Cowe, who during my absence had returned from the chace [chase or hunt]. The remainder of this day I spent in observations in and about the town, reviewing my specimens, &c.

The town of Cowe consists of about one hundred dwellings, near the banks of the Tanase, on both sides of the river.

The Cherokees construct their habitations on a different plan from the Creeks; that is, but one oblong four square building, of one story high; the materials consisting of logs or trunks of trees, stripped of their bark, notched at their ends, fixed one upon another, and afterwards plaistered well, both inside and out, with clay well tempered with dry grass, and the whole covered or roofed with the bark of the chesnut tree or long broad shingles. This building is however partitioned transversely, forming three apartments, which communicate with each other by inside doors; each house or habitation has besides a little conical house, covered with dirt, which is called the winter or hot-house; this stands a few yards distance from the mansion-house, opposite the front door.

The council or town-house is a large rotunda, capable of accommodating several hundred people: it stands on the top of an ancient artificial mount of earth, of about twenty feet perpendicular, and the rotunda on the top of it being above thirty feet more, gives the whole fabric an elevation of about sixty feet from the common surface of the ground. But it may be proper to observe, that this mount on which the rotunda stands, is of a much ancienter date than the building, and perhaps was raised for another purpose. The Cherokees themselves are as ignorant as we are, by what people or for what purpose these artificial hills were raised; they have various stories concerning them, the best of which amount to no more than mere conjecture, and leave us entirely in the dark; but they have a tradition common with the other nations of Indians, that they found them in much the same condition as they now appear, when their forefathers arrived from the West and possessed themselves of the country, after vanquishing the nations of red men who then inhabited it, who themselves found these mounts when they took possession of the country, the former possessors delivering the same story concerning them: perhaps they were designed and apropriated by the people who constructed them, to some religious purpose, as great altars and temples similar to the high places and sacred groves anciently amongst the Canaanites and other nations of Palestine and Judea.

The rotunda is constructed after the following manner: they first fix in the ground a circular range of posts or trunks of trees, about six feet high, at equal distances, which are notched at top, to receive into them from one to another, a range of beams or wall plates; within this is another circular order of very large and strong pillars, above twelve feet high, notched in like manner at top, to receive another range of wall plates; and within this is yet another or third range of stronger and higher pillars, but fewer in number, and standing at a greater distance from each other; and lastly, in the centre stands a very strong pillar, which forms the pinnacle of the building, and to which the rafters centre at top; these rafters are strengthened and bound together by cross beams and laths, which sustain the roof or covering, which is a layer of bark neatly placed, and tight enough to exclude the rain, and sometimes they cast a thin superficies of earth over all. There is but one large door, which serves at the same time to admit light from without and the smoak to escape when a fire is kindled; but as there is but a small fire kept, sufficient to give light at night, and that fed with dry small sound wood divested of its bark, there is but little smoak. All around the inside of the building, betwixt the second range of pillars and the wall, is a range of cabins or sophas, consisting of two or three steps, one above or behind the other, in theatrical order, where the assembly sit or lean down; these sophas are covered with mats or carpets, very curiously made of thin splints of Ash or Oak, woven or platted together; near the great pillar in the centre the fire is kindled for light, near which the musicians seat themselves, and round about this the performers exhibit their dances and other shows at public festivals, which happen almost every night throughout the year.

About the close of the evening I accompanied Mr. Galahan and other white traders to the rotunda, where was a grand festival, music and dancing. This assembly was held principally to rehearse the ball-play dance, this town being challenged to play against another the next day.

The people being assembled and seated in order, and the musicians having taken their station, the ball opens, first with a long harangue or oration, spoken by an aged chief, in commendation of the manly exercise of the ball-play, recounting the many and brilliant victories which the town of Cowe had gained over the other towns in the nation, not forgetting or neglecting to recite his own exploits, together with those of other aged men now present, coadjutors in the performance of these athletic games in their youthful days.

This oration was delivered with great spirit and eloquence, and was meant to influence the passions of the young men present, excite them to emulation and inspire them with ambition.

This prologue being at an end, the musicians began, both vocal and instrumental; when presently a company of girls, hand in hand, dressed in clean white robes and ornamented with beads, bracelets and a profusion of gay ribbands, entering the door, immediately began to sing their responses in a gentle, low, and sweet voice, and formed themselves in a semicircular file or line, in two ranks, back to back, facing the spectators and musicians, moving slowly round and round. This continued about a quarter of an hour, when we were surprised by a sudden very loud and shrill whoop, uttered at once by a company of young fellows, who came in briskly after one another, with rackets or hurls in one hand. These champions likewise were well dressed, painted, and ornamented with silver bracelets, gorgets [large shell, stone, or metal ornaments worn around the neck] and wampum, neatly ornamented with moccasins and high waving plumes in their diadems: they immediately formed themselves in a semicircular rank also, in front of the girls, when these changed their order, and formed a single rank parallel to the men, raising their voices in responses to the tunes of the young champions, the semicircles continually moving round. There was something singular and diverting in their step and motions, and I imagine not to be learned to exactness but with great attention and perseverance. The step, if it can be so termed, was performed after the following manner; first, the motion began at one end of the semicircle, gently rising up and down upon their toes and heels alternately, when the first was up on tip-toe, the next began to raise the heel, and by the time the first rested again on the heel, the second was on tip-toe, thus from one end of the rank to the other, so that some were always up and some down, alternately and regularly, without the least baulk or confusion; and they at the same time, and in the same motion, moved on obliquely or sideways, so that the circle performed a double or complex motion in its progression, and at stated times exhibited a grand or universal movement, instantly and unexpectedly to the spectators, by each rank turning to right and left, taking each others places: the movements were managed with inconceivable alertness and address, and accompanied with an instantaneous and universal elevation of the voice, and shrill whoop.

The Cherokees, besides the ball-play dance, have a variety of others equally entertaining. The men especially exercise themselves with a variety of gesticulations and capers, some of which are ludicrous and diverting enough; and they have others which are of the martial order, and others of the chace; these seem to be somewhat of a tragical nature, wherein they exhibit astonishing feats of military prowess, masculine strength and activity. Indeed all their dances and musical entertainments seem to be theatrical exhibitions or plays, varied with comic and sometimes lascivious interludes: the women however conduct themselves with a very becoming grace and decency, insomuch that in amorous interludes, when their responses and gestures seem consenting to natural liberties, they veil themselves, just discovering a glance of their sparkling eyes and blushing faces, expressive of sensibility.

Next morning early I set off on my return, and meeting with no material occurrences on the road, in two days arrived safe at Keowe, where I tarried two or three days, employed in augmenting my collections of specimens, and waiting for Mr. Galahan, who was to call on me here, to accompany him to Sinica, where he and other traders were to meet Mr. Cameron, the deputy-commissary, to hold a congress at that town, with the chiefs of the Lower Cherokees, to consult preliminaries introductory to a general congress and treaty with these Indians, which was to be convened next June, and held in the Overhill towns.

I observed in the environs of Keowe, on the bases of the rocky hills, immediately ascending from the low grounds near the river bank, a great number of very singular antiquities, the work of the ancients; they seem to me to have been altars for sacrifice or sepulchers: they were constructed of four flat stones, two set on an edge for the sides, one closed one end, and a very large flat one lay horizontally at top, so that the other end was open; this fabric was four or five feet in length, two feet high, and three in width. I inquired of the trader what they were, who could not tell me certainly, but supposed them to be ancient Indian ovens; the Indians can give no account of them: they are on the surface of the ground, and are of different dimensions.

I accompanied the traders to Sinica, where we found the commissary and the Indian chiefs convened in counsel: continued at Sinica some time, employing myself in observations, and making collections of every thing worthy of notice: and finding the Indians to be yet unsettled in their determination, and not in a good humour, I abandoned the project of visiting the regions beyond the Cherokee mountains for this season; set off for my return to fort James, Dartmouth, lodged this night in the forests near the banks of a delightful large creek, a branch of Keowe river, and next day arrived safe at Dartmouth.[3]

List of towns and villages in the Cherokee nation inhabited at this day, viz.

No.	1 Echoe		
	2 Nucase	On the Tanase East of the Jore mountains.	
	3 Whatoga		4 towns
	4 Cowe		

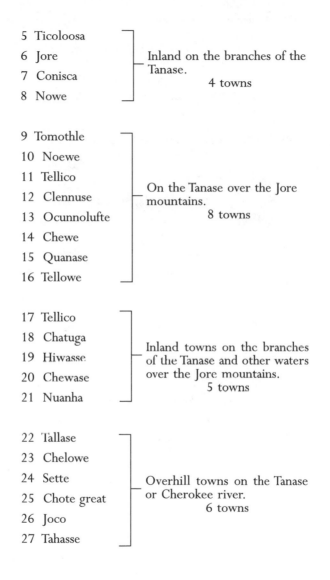

5	Ticoloosa	
6	Jore	Inland on the branches of the Tanase.
7	Conisca	
8	Nowe	4 towns

9	Tomothle	
10	Noewe	
11	Tellico	
12	Clennuse	On the Tanase over the Jore mountains.
13	Ocunnolufte	8 towns
14	Chewe	
15	Quanase	
16	Tellowe	

17	Tellico	
18	Chatuga	Inland towns on the branches of the Tanase and other waters over the Jore mountains.
19	Hiwasse	
20	Chewase	
21	Nuanha	5 towns

22	Tallase	
23	Chelowe	
24	Sette	Overhill towns on the Tanase or Cherokee river.
25	Chote great	6 towns
26	Joco	
27	Tahasse	

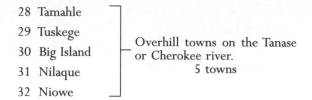

28 Tamahle	
29 Tuskege	
30 Big Island	Overhill towns on the Tanase or Cherokee river.
31 Nilaque	5 towns
32 Niowe	

Lower towns East of the mountains, viz.

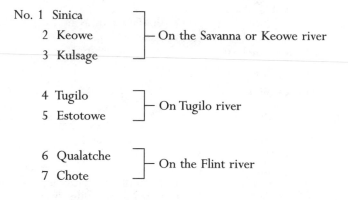

No. 1 Sinica	
2 Keowe	On the Savanna or Keowe river
3 Kulsage	

4 Tugilo	
5 Estotowe	On Tugilo river

6 Qualatche	
7 Chote	On the Flint river

Towns on the waters of other rivers
Estotowe great. Allagae. Jore. Nae oche.
In all forty-three towns.[4]

Too Near the Shore, 1780

❧·❦·❧·❦·❧·❦·❧·❦·❧·❦·❧·❦·❧·❦·❧·❦·❧·❦·❧·❦·❧·❦·❧·❦·❧·❦·❧·❦·❧·❦

Around the time of the American Revolution, relations between Indians and the colonists were at the boiling point.

As a result of the Sycamore Shoals Treaty in 1775, many
Cherokee lands were sold to Richard Henderson and Nathaniel
Hart, the representatives of the Transylvania Company. A group
of disfranchised Cherokees under the leadership of Tsiyugunsini,
or Dragging Canoe, broke off from the main body of Cherokees. Siding with the British during the Revolution, they attacked American forces and frontier settlements. In retribu-
tion, the Americans attacked Cherokee towns. In March 1777,
many homeless Cherokees followed Dragging Canoe to new
settlements on Chickamauga Creek in present-day Hamilton

County, Tennessee, where they were later joined by more Cherokees, Creeks, Tories, and black slave refugees. This group became known as the Chickamaugans.[1]

In April 1779, a group of Virginia and North Carolina volunteers ransacked and burned the Chickamauga villages and carried off twenty thousand bushels of corn. This occurred while many of the warriors were off fighting for the British along the Georgia and South Carolina borders. Rather than rebuild on the burned town sites, Dragging Canoe established five new towns farther down the Tennessee River.[2] It was from these five Lower Towns that the Chickamaugans launched their initial attacks on the John Donelson party.

John Donelson was a Virginia surveyor who purchased land along the Cumberland River from Richard Henderson. In November 1779, James Robertson joined Donelson in an effort to settle the Cumberland River tracts. The plan called for Robertson to take the overland route, leading a group of single men, older male children, skilled hunters, livestock, and packhorses to the region near the southern bend of the Cumberland known as Big Salt Lick or French Salt Springs. Donelson would leave in December and travel by water, leading the women, servants, and younger children aboard thirty flatboats from Fort Patrick Henry on the Holston River. The two groups would rejoin at Big Salt Lick. Traveling with Donelson was his daughter Rachel, who later married Andrew Jackson.[3]

Donelson's classic journal of his river voyage is a tale of severe hardship. His party had barely departed when it was delayed for two months by low water. Then it had to deal with freezing conditions, smallpox, and attacks by the Chickamaugans from shore.

When Donelson's party finally completed the journey to Big Salt Lick, it reunited with Robertson's group to found what is now Nashville, Tennessee. Donelson went on to establish a home, Clover Bottom, on the Stone's River. He had only a few years to enjoy it before he was killed by Indians while on a business trip.[4]

The excerpt below, taken from Donelson's journal, tells of his struggles to negotiate the river through territory controlled by Dragging Canoe's Chickamaugans. The footnote in the excerpt explains the fate of some of the less fortunate members of the party. It was added by historian J. G. M. Ramsey seventy years after the journal was written. *Goodspeed's General History of Tennessee*, published in 1887, reported that the Chickamaugans caught smallpox from the captives of the Stuart boat and suffered great mortality as a result.[5]

Excerpts from Journal of a Voyage, intended by God's permission, in the good boat Adventure, from Fort Patrick Henry on Holston River, to the French Salt Springs on Cumberland River, kept by John Donaldson *[Donelson]*

Tuesday, [March] 7th [1780].—Got under way very early, the day proving very windy, a S.S.W. [south-southwest wind], and the river being wide occasioned a high sea, insomuch that some of the smaller crafts were in danger; therefore came to, at the uppermost Chiccamauga Town, which was then evacuated, where we lay by that afternoon and camped that night. The wife of Ephraim Peyton was here delivered of a child. Mr. Peyton has gone through by land with Capt. Robertson.

Wednesday, 8th.——Cast off at 10 o'clock, and proceed down to an Indian village, which was inhabited, on the south side of the river; they insisted on us to "come ashore," called us brothers, and showed other signs of friendship, insomuch that Mr. John Caffrey and my son then on board took a canoe which I had in tow, and were crossing over to them, the rest of the fleet having landed on the opposite shore. After they had gone some distance, a half-breed, who called himself Archy Coody with several other Indians, jumped into a canoe, met them, and advised them to return to the boat, which they did, together with Coody and several canoes which left the shore and followed directly after him. They appeared to be friendly. After distributing some presents among them, with which they seemed much pleased, we observed a number of Indians on the other side embarking in their canoes, armed and painted with red and black. Coody immediately made signs to his companions, ordering them to quit the boat, which they did, himself and another Indian remaining with us and telling us to move off instantly. We had not gone far before we discovered a number of Indians armed and painted proceeding down the river, as it were, to intercept us. Coody, the half-breed, and his companion, sailed with us for some time, and telling us that we had passed all the towns and were out of danger, left us. But we had not gone far until we had come in sight of another town, situated likewise on the south side of the river, nearly opposite a small island. Here they again invited us to come on shore, called us brothers, and observing the boats standing off for the opposite channel, told us that "their side of the river was better for boats to pass." And here we must regret the unfortunate death of young Mr. Payne, on board Capt. Blackemore's boat, who was mortally wounded by reason of the boat running too near the northern shore opposite the town, where some of the enemy lay concealed, and the more tragical misfortune of poor Stuart, his family and friends to the number of twenty-eight persons. This man had embarked with us for the Western country, but his family being diseased with the small pox, it was agreed upon between him and the company that he should keep at some distance in the rear, for fear of the infection spreading, and he was warned each night when the encampment should take place by the sound of a horn. After we had passed the town, the Indians having now collected to a considerable number, observing his helpless situation, singled off from the rest of the fleet, intercepted him and killed and took prisoners the whole crew, to the great grief of the whole company, uncertain how soon they might share the same fate; their cries were distinctly heard by those boats in the rear.

We still perceived them marching down the river in considerable bodies, keeping pace with us until the Cumberland Mountain withdrew them from our sight, when we were in hopes we had escaped them. We were now arrived at the place called the Whirl or Suck, where the river is compressed within less than half its common width above, by the Cumberland Mountain, which juts in on both sides. In passing through the upper part of these narrows, at a place described by Coody, which he termed the "boiling pot," a trivial accident had nearly ruined the expedition. One of the company, John Cotton, who was moving down in a large canoe, had attached it to Robert Cartwright's boat, into which he and his family had gone for safety. The canoe was here overturned, and the little cargo lost. The company pitying his distress, concluded to halt and assist him in recovering his property. They had landed on the northern shore at a level spot, and were going up to the place, when the Indians, to our astonishment, appeared immediately over us on the opposite cliffs, and commenced firing down upon us, which occasioned a precipitate retreat to the boats. We immediately moved off, the Indians lining the bluffs along continued their fire from the heights on our boats below, without doing any other injury than wounding four slightly. Jennings's boat is missing.

We have now passed through the Whirl. The river widens with a placid and gentle current; and all the company appear to be in safety except the family of Jonathan Jennings, whose boat ran on a large rock, projecting out from the northern shore, and partly immersed in water immediately at the Whirl, where we were compelled to leave them, perhaps to be slaughtered by their merciless enemies. Continued to sail on that day and floated throughout the following night.

Thursday, 9th.——Proceeded on our journey, nothing happening worthy attention to-day; floated till about midnight, and encamped on the northern shore.

Friday, 10th.——This morning about 4 o'clock we were surprised by the cries of "help poor Jennings," at some distance in the rear. He had discovered us by our fires, and came up in the most wretched condition. He states, that as soon as the Indians discovered his situation they turned their whole attention to him, and kept up a most galling fire at his boat. He ordered his wife, a son nearly grown, a young man who accompanied them, and his negro man and woman, to throw all his goods into the river, to lighten their boat for the purpose of getting her off, himself returning their fire as well as he could, being a good soldier and an excellent marksman. But before they had accomplished their object, his son, the young man and the negro, jumped out of the boat and left them. He thinks the young man and the negro were wounded before they left the boat.* Mrs. Jennings, however, and the negro woman, succeeded in unloading the boat, but chiefly by the exertions of Mrs. Jennings, who got out of the boat and shoved her off, but was near falling a victim to her own intrepidity on account of the boat starting so suddenly as soon as loosened from the rock. Upon examination, he appears to have made a wonderful escape, for his boat is pierced in numberless places with bullets. It is to be remarked, that Mrs. Peyton, who was the night before delivered of an infant, which was unfortunately killed upon the hurry and confusion consequent upon such a disaster, assisted them, being frequently exposed to wet and cold then and afterwards, and that her health appears to be good at this time, and I think and hope she will do well. Their clothes were very much cut with bullets, especially Mrs. Jennings's.

Saturday, 11th.——Got under way after having distributed the family of Mrs. Jennings in the other boats. Rowed on quietly that day, and encamped for the night on the north shore.

Sunday, 12th.——Set out, and after a few hour's sailing we heard the crowing of cocks, and soon came within view of the town; here they fired on us again without doing any injury.

After running until about 10 o'clock, came in sight of the Muscle Shoals. Halted on the northern shore at the appearance of the shoals, in order to search for the signs Capt. James Robertson was to make for us at that place. He set out from Holston early in the fall of 1779, was to proceed by the way of Kentucky to the Big Salt Lick on Cumberland River, with several others in company, was to come across from the Big Salt Lick to the upper end of the shoals, there to make such signs that we might know he had been there, and that it was practicable for us to go across by land. But to our great mortification we can find none—from which we conclude that it would not be prudent to make the attempt, and are determined, knowing ourselves to be in such imminent danger, to pursue our journey down the river. After trimming our boats in the best manner possible, we ran through the shoals before night. When we approached them they had a dreadful appearance to those who had never seen them before. The water being high made a terrible roaring, which could be heard at some distance among the drift-wood heaped frightfully upon the points of the islands, the current running in every possible direction. Here we did not know how soon we should be dashed to pieces, and all our troubles ended at once. Our boats frequently dragged on the bottom, and appeared constantly in danger of striking. They warped as much as in a rough sea. But by the hand of Providence we are now preserved from this danger also. I know not the length of this wonderful shoal; it had been represented to me to be 25 or 30 miles. If so, we must have descended very rapidly, as indeed we did, for we passed it in about three hours. Came to, and camped on the northern shore, not far below the shoals, for the night.

Monday, 13th.——Got under way early in the morning and made a good run that day.

Tuesday, 14th.——Set out early. On this day two boats approaching too near the shore, were fired on by the Indians. Five of the crews were wounded, but not dangerously. Came to camp at night near the mouth of a creek. After kindling fires and preparing for rest, the company were alarmed, on account of the incessant barking our dogs kept up; taking it for granted that the Indians were attempting to surprise us, we retreated precipitately to the boats; fell down the river about a mile and encamped on the other shore. In the morning I prevailed on Mr. Caffrey and my son to cross below in a canoe, and return to the place; which they did, and found an

African negro we had left in the hurry, asleep by one of the fires. The voyagers returned and collected their utensils which had been left.

Wednesday, 15th.——Got under way and moved on peaceably the five following days, when we arrived at the mouth of the Tennessee on Monday, the 20th, and landed on the lower point immediately on the bank of the Ohio. Our situation here is truly disagreeable. The river is very high, and the current rapid, our boats not constructed for the purpose of stemming a rapid stream, our provision exhausted, the crews almost worn down with hunger and fatigue, and know not what distance we have to go, or what time it will take us to our place of destination. The scene is rendered still more melancholy, as several boats will not attempt to ascend the rapid current. Some intend to descend the Mississippi to Natchez; others are bound for the Illinois——among the rest my son-in-law and daughter. We now part, perhaps to meet no more, for I am determined to pursue my course, happen what will. . . .

Friday, 31st.——Set out this day, and after running some distance, met with Col. Richard Henderson, who was running the line between Virginia and North-Carolina. At this meeting we were much rejoiced. He gave us every information we wished, and further informed us that he had purchased a quantity of corn in Kentucky, to be shipped at the Falls of Ohio for the use of the Cumberland settlement. We are now without bread, and are compelled to hunt the buffalo to preserve life. Worn out with fatigue, our progress at present is slow. Camped at night near the mouth of a little river, at which place and below there is a handsome bottom of rich land. Here we found a pair of hand-mill stones set up for grinding, but appeared not to have been used for a great length of time.

Proceeded on quietly until the 12th of April, at which time we came to the mouth of a little river running in on the north side, by Moses Renfoe and his company called Red River, up which they intend to settle. Here they took leave of us. We proceeded up Cumberland, nothing happening material until the 23d, when we reached the first settlement on the north side of the river, one mile and a half below the Big Salt Lick and called Eaton's Station, after a man of that name, who with several other families, came through Kentucky and settled there.

Monday, April 24th.—This day we arrived at our journey's end at the Big Salt Lick, where we have the pleasure of finding Capt. Robertson and his company. It is a source of satisfaction to us to be enabled to restore to him and others their families and friends, who were entrusted to our care, and who, sometime since, perhaps, despaired of ever meeting again. Though our prospects at present are dreary, we have found a few log cabins which have been built on a cedar bluff above the Lick, by Capt. Robertson and his company.

* The negro was drowned. The son and the young man swam to the north side of the river, where they found and embarked in a canoe

and floated down the river. The next day they were met by five canoes full of Indians, who took them prisoners and carried them to Chickamauga, where they killed and burned the young man. They knocked Jennings down and were about to kill him, but were prevented by the friendly mediation of Rogers, an Indian trader, who ransomed him with goods. Rogers had been taken prisoner by Sevier a short time before, and had been released; and that good office he requited by the ransom of Jennings.[6]

A PIPE AND A LITTLE TOBACCO, 1785

❖◄❖◄❖◄❖◄❖◄❖◄❖◄❖◄❖◄❖◄❖◄❖◄❖◄◄◄◄◄❖◄

The Cherokee chief Corn Tassel was known by many different names. His Cherokee name is given as Rayetaeh on the Treaty
of Long Island and as Koatohce on the Treaty of Hopewell. He
was also called Kaallahnor, Udsidasata, Tassel, Old Tassel, and
Kahn-yah-tah-hee, or the First to Kill.[1] Sequoyah, or George Gist,
the inventor of the Cherokee alphabet, was the son of Corn
Tassel's sister. Corn Tassel was known for his honesty and reso-
luteness and for seeking the best for his people through his peace
efforts. He is described as being stout, round-faced, and mild-
mannered.[2]

The following excerpt includes speeches made by Corn Tassel at the Treaty of Hopewell talks, held in November 1785. This

was the first treaty between the young United States and the Cherokees. By signing this treaty, the Cherokees accepted the protection of the United States, gained the right to send a representative to Congress, agreed to exchange prisoners and to allow the United States to regulate trade, agreed on the boundaries of the Cherokee lands, and received promises that no whites would be allowed to settle on their lands.[3]

Although this was a promising agreement for the Cherokees, the terms of the Treaty of Hopewell didn't last long. Several months later, Corn Tassel and Hanging Maw were forced to sign the so-called Treaty of Coyatee at virtual gunpoint. Under that treaty, the Cherokees were forced to surrender what remained of their lands north of the Little Tennessee River.[4]

In 1788, Corn Tassel, his son, and several other chiefs, including Hanging Maw's brother Abram, were murdered by some of John Sevier's men at a meeting at Abram's house. The meeting had been called by Sevier's militia and was held under a flag of truce.[5]

Also present at the Treaty of Hopewell was the war woman of Chota, Nancy Ward. Her bravery in battle against the Creek Indians years earlier had earned her the title of Ghighau, or Beloved Woman. Respected women were often allowed into the predominately male Cherokee council house. These women played important roles in the tribe and could at times override the authority of the male council.[6] Among the other headmen present at the Treaty of Hopewell were Unsuckanail, representing three Middle Towns, and Chescoenwhee, Tuckasee, and

Oonanootee, representing other Cherokee towns.[7]

During the treaty meeting, the Cherokees presented the commissioners with gifts as a sign of friendship and good faith. The gifts are described in the treaty records and are shown here at the places in the talks when they were presented.

The "B. H." who signed the footnotes to the talks at Hopewell was probably the mixed-blood Indian agent Benjamin Hawkins.

Excerpts from talks at the Treaty of Hopewell

NOVEMBER 22 [1785]

The commissioners assembled. Present: Benjamin Hawkins, Andrew Pickens, Joseph Martin, and Laughlin McIntosh. From the State of North Carolina, William Blount, agent. From the State of Georgia, John King and Thomas Glasscock, commissioners. From all the tribes or towns of the Cherokees, the head-men and warriors. James Madison, Arthur Coody, interpreters.

The commissioners delivered the following address to the Indians:

Head-men and warriors of all the Cherokees: We are the men whom you were informed came from Congress to meet you, the head-men and warriors of all the Cherokees, to give you peace, and to receive you into the favor and protection of the United States; and to remove, as far as may be, all causes of future contention or quarrels. That you, your people, your wives and children, may be happy, and feel and know the blessings of the new change of sovereignty over this land, which you and we inhabit.

We sincerely wish you to live as happily as we do ourselves, and to promote that happiness as far as is in our power, regardless of any distinction of color, or of any difference in our customs, our manners, or particular situation.

This humane and generous act of the United States, will no doubt be received by you with gladness, and held in grateful remembrance, and the more so, as many of your young men, and the greatest number of your warriors, during the late war, were our enemies, and assisted the King of Great Britain in his endeavors to conquer our country.

You, yourselves, know, that you refused to listen to the good talks Congress sent you; that the cause you espoused was a bad one; that all the adherents of the King of Great Britain are compelled to leave this country, never more to return.

Congress is now the sovereign of all our country, which we now point out to you on the map.* They want none of your lands, or any thing else which belongs to you; and as an earnest of their regard for you, we propose to enter into articles of a treaty perfectly equal, and conformable to what we now tell you.

If you have any grievances to complain of, we will hear them, and take such measures, in consequence thereof, as may be proper. We expect you will speak your minds freely, and look upon us as the representatives of your father and friend, the Congress, who will see justice done you. You may now retire, and reflect on what we have told you, and let us hear from you to-morrow, or as soon as possible.

November 23

Present as yesterday. After sitting some time in silence, the Tassel of Chota arose, and addressed the commissioners as follows:

I am going to let the commissioners hear what I have to say to them. I told you yesterday I would do this today. I was very much pleased at the talk you gave us yesterday; it is very different from what I expected when I left home; the headmen and warriors are also equally pleased with it.

Now, I shall give you my own talk. I am made of this earth, on which the great man above placed me, to possess it; and what I am about to tell you, I have had in my mind for many years.

This land we are now on, is the land we were fighting for, during the late contest,† and the great man made it for us to subsist upon. You must know the red people are the aborigines of this land, and that it is but a few years since the white people found it out. I am of the first stock, as the commissioners know, and a native of this land; and the white people are now living on it as our friends. From the beginning of the first friendship between the white and red people, beads were given as an emblem thereof: and these are the beads I give to the commissioners of the United States, as a confirmation of our friendship, and as a proof of my opinion of what you yesterday told us. (A string of white beads)

The commissioners have heard how the white people have encroached on our lands, on every side of us that they could approach.

I remember the talks I delivered at the Long Island of Holston, and I remember giving our lands to Colonel Christie and others, who treated with us, and in a manner compelled me thereto, in 1777. I remember the talks to Colonel Christie, when I gave the lands at the mouth of Cloud's creek, eighteen springs past. At that treaty, we agreed upon the line near the mouth of Lime Stone. The Virginia line, and part from the mouth of Cloud's creek to Cumberland mountain, near the gap, was paid for by Virginia.

From Cloud's creek, a direct line to the Chimney-top mountain, thence, to the mouth of Big Lime Stone, on Nolichucky, thence, to the first mountain about six miles from the river, on a line across the sun, was never paid for by the Carolina which joins the Virginia line. I wish the commissioners to know every thing that concerns us, as I tell nothing but the truth. They, the people of North Carolina, have taken our lands for no consideration, and are now making their fortunes out of them. I have informed the commissioners of the line I gave up, and the people of North Carolina and Virginia have gone over it, and encroached on our lands expressly against our inclination. They have gone over the line near Little River, and they have gone over Nine-mile Creek, which is but nine miles from our towns. I am glad of this opportunity of getting redress from the commissioners. If Congress had not interposed, I and my people must have moved. They have even marked the lands on the bank of the river near the town where I live; and from thence, down in the fork of the Tennessee and Holston.

I have given in to you a detail of the abuse and encroachments of these two States. We shall be satisfied if we are paid for the lands we have given up, but we will not, nor cannot, give up any more—I mean the line I gave to Colonel Christie.

I have no more to say, but one of our beloved women has, who has born and raised up warriors. (A string of beads)

The War-woman of Chota then addressed the commissioners:

I am fond of hearing that there is a peace, and I hope you have now taken us by the hand in real friendship. I have a pipe and a little tobacco to give the commissioners to smoke in friendship. I look on you and the red people as my children. Your having determined on peace is most pleasing to me, for I have seen much trouble during the late war. I am old, but I hope yet to bear children, who will grow up and people our nation, as we are now to be under the protection of Congress, and shall have no more disturbance. (A string, little old pipe, and some tobacco)

The talk I have given, is from the young warriors I have raised in my town, as well as myself. They rejoice that we have peace, and we hope the chain of friendship will never more be broke. (A string of beads)

THE COMMISSIONERS TO THE TASSEL. We want the boundary of your country; you must recollect yourself and give it to us, particularly the line between you and the citizens, with any information you have on that subject. If necessary, you may consult your friends, and inform us to-morrow, or as soon as possible with conveniency.

TASSEL. I will let you know the line to-morrow. I have done speaking for this day.

UNSUCKANAIL, OF NEW-CUSSE, IN THE MIDDLE SETTLEMENT. I speak in behalf of Kowé, New-Cusse, and Watoge. I am much pleased with the talks between the commissioners, and the Tassel, who is the beloved man of Chota. I remember the talks given out by you yesterday. I shall always, I hope, remember, that if we were distressed in any manner, we should make our complaints to the commissioners, that justice may be done. There are around us young men and warriors, who hear our talks, and who are interested in the succes of this treaty, particularly as their lands are taken from them, on which they lived entirely by hunting. And I hope, and they all anxiously hope, it is in the power of the commissioners to do them justice. The line mentioned by the beloved man of Chota, is in truth, as he expressed it; I remember it, and it was formerly our hunting grounds.

The encroachments on this side of the line have entirely deprived us of our hunting grounds; and I hope the commissioners will remove the white people to their own side. This is the desire of the three towns I speak for; the settlements I mean are those on Pigeon river and Swananno. It was the desire of the commissioners that the Indians should tell all their grievances, and I hope they will do justly therein. When any of my young men are hunting on their own grounds, and meet the white people, order them off and claim our deer. (A string of white beads)

CHESCOENWHEE. I am well satisfied with the talks of this day; I intended to speak, but as the day is far spent, I will decline it till to-morrow. I will go home and consider on it.

NOVEMBER 24

Present as yesterday:

TUCKASEE. I remember the talks when I made peace. I have appointed Chescoenwhee to speak for me to-day.

CHESCOENWHEE. I rejoice that the commissioners have delivered their talks to the head-men of the different towns. I am in hopes that these our talks will always remain unbroken. What you hear from the representatives of the towns, the young warriors will invariably adhere to. I am in hopes it is now in the power of the commissioners, from their talks of yesterday and the day before, to see justice done to us; to see that we may yet have a little land to hunt upon; I was sent here to settle all matters respecting my country, and being under the protection of the United States, I shall return satisfied: we have been formerly under the protection of Great Britain, and then, when I saw a white man, I esteemed him a friend, and I hope that the commissioners of Congress will see that times may be as formerly. I wish what I say may be deemed strictly true, for so it is, and that I may be always looked on as a friend to the thirteen United States, and that they will see justice done me.

The talks of the commissioners are the most pleasing to us, as they do not want any lands. Formerly, when I had peace talks, the first thing the white people expressed, was a desire for our lands. I am in hopes you will adjust and settle our limits, so that we may be secured in the possession of our own. I will abide by what hitherto has been said on this subject, but cannot cede any more lands. (A string of beads)

I am in hopes the commissioners will deliver to us our prisoners who are in their lands. Neither the commissioners, nor any of the citizens of the United States, can suppose that we can be at peace on their account; they are our own flesh and blood, and we desire them out of your country. I am in hopes of seeing them with the assistance of the commissioners, they have been long detained, and we often were promised by colonel Martin that we should see them. One of them was taken from Talksoa, three girls and one boy from Erejoy, and one boy from Tuckareechée; we do not know how old they are; we are a people who do not know how to count by years; they are in North Carolina, and were taken by an army from thence.

OONANOOTEE. I am to deliver the talks in answer to what

I heard at Oostanawie. I was sent down from different towns to receive the talks of the commissioners, and to be governed by them. I do expect, by the time I return home from the commissioners, the young men of the towns of our nation will be there to hear me repeat what you have or shall say to me. I was told by all of them, when I set out, that they expected I would return with good talks. It was the desire of the commissioners, that we should tell all our grievances; the encroachment on our hunting grounds is the source of all ours, and I hope they can and will take measures to see justice done in our land. I have attended to the talks of the commissioners, and our beloved men, and I sincerely wish they may always abide by them. I am in hopes it is in your power to see our distresses redressed, and that you will order off the people who are settled on our lands, and protect for us our hunting grounds. (A string of beads)

I wish the commissioners to take in hand the case of the traders in our country, and settle what respects them during the late war, so that they may not be seized on and plundered by bodies of armed men as they pass to and from the nation. I am come down as one to make peace with the commissioners of the United States of America, and I hope the traders may pass through the country. I wish the commissioners would prevent such acts of injustice as robbing the traders; several of them have been plundered in Georgia and South Carolina, and their lives endangered if they should attempt to recover their property. As for my part; I mean to keep the path clear for the traders, as far as our line, and I hope the commissioners will do the same on their part. Here are the chiefs of all our nation, who hear me; the traders have been out for goods and returned without any, having been robbed, and I hope it will not be the case again. I sincerely desire that our talks and complaints may go up to Congress, that they may know how we are distressed about our country. I have delivered the talks to the commissioners, and laid the beads on the beloved table, and as to my part of the country, I will keep the path clear.

TASSEL. We have said all we intend to day; if the commissioners have any thing to say, we will hear it, and answer them.

COMMISSIONERS. We want the boundary of your country, particularly to the northward and eastward; this we told you yesterday; when we can agree upon the bounds of the lands, we mean to allot to you, we will prepare the draught of a treaty on the plan we mentioned to you in our address.

TASSEL. I expected to give the bounds of our country, but it is too late in the day, and I will do it to-morrow.

* We used McMurray's map, and explained, with great pains, the limits of the United States as well as the occurrences of the late war; and we believe they comprehend us. Some of the Indians had visited the Six Nations; some had been up the Wabash and down the Miami, to lake Erie; and others had been at fort Pitt, the Natchez, Pensacola, St. Augustine, Savannah, Charleston, and Wiliamsburg.   B. H.

†Hopewell is fifteen miles above the junction of the Keowee and Tugalo; it is a seat of General Pickens, in sight of Seneca, an Indian

town at the commencement of the late war, inhabited by one hundred gun-men, but at present a waste. Dewit's corner is forty miles east of this, and that was the eastern Indian boundary, till the treaty of 1777. B. H.[8]

Blood is Spilt at Both of Our Houses, 1793

➤-◄-➤-◄-➤-◄-➤-◄-➤-◄-➤-◄-➤-◄-➤-◄-➤-◄-➤-◄-➤-◄-➤-◄-➤-◄-➤-◄

Hanging Maw, also known as Scholauetta or Hanging Man, was a principal leader of the Cherokees in the late eighteenth century.[1] He participated in the Treaty of Holston in 1791, at which several Cherokee leaders were duped into ceding extensive territory in East Tennessee and western North Carolina for a yearly annuity of one thousand dollars and a few supplies.[2]

In 1792 and 1793, Chickamauga Cherokees made attacks on white settlements at the instigation of the Spanish. In an effort to restore peace, William Blount, governor of the Southwest Territory, called a meeting of Cherokee leaders at Hanging Maw's home in Coyatee. Before departing the territory for

Philadelphia, Blount dispatched Captain John Beard to bring some murderers to justice. In the governor's absence, Beard violated his orders by leading an attack on Hanging Maw's home while the Cherokees and whites were assembled there at Blount's request.[3]

After the attack, the Cherokees waited for the government to capture Beard. When it was clear the justice they had been promised was not forthcoming, the Cherokees retaliated.

In a report dated December 13, 1793, Secretary of War Henry Knox expressed his frustration over the outbreak of war in the Southwest:

> A party of armed men, under Captain John Beard, who had been called into service by Governor Blount, with a view of protecting the settlers, did, on the 12th of June, in defiance of their orders, cross the Tennessee, and surprise and kill a number of our best friends among the Indians, at the moment Governor Blount's messengers were among them.
>
> This violent outrage, so disgraceful to the United States, has been followed by several others, and the Southwestern Territory is involved in a war with the Cherokees; which, as it relates to the above event, must be considered as highly unjust. It is to be apprehended and regretted, that, from the prejudice against Indians on the frontiers, it is but too probable that the perpetrators of these violences will escape unpunished. Such measures as the laws authorize have been directed, but, as yet, no result has been transmitted.
>
> Great bodies of militia have been brought into service

on this occasion, in order to guard against the effects of savage retaliation. Much expense has been already incurred, nor is it yet terminated: for, however hostilities shall be restrained by the severity of the winter, yet they may be expected to break out with renewed violence in the spring.

The evil seems to require a remedy; but no Indian peace will be permanent, unless an effectual mode can be devised to punish the violators of it on both sides. It will be with an ill grace that the United States demand the punishment of banditti Indians, when, at the same time, the guilty whites escape with impunity.[4]

Finally, in November 1794, Cherokees under Hanging Maw and Chickamauga leader John Watts met with Blount at the Tellico Blockhouse and reached a peace agreement. The pledge of John Watts to give up his warlike actions against the whites signaled the end of organized Cherokee military resistance against the United States. Another Chickamauga leader, Doublehead, would make a few more attacks on the whites, but those soon subsided.

Hanging Maw did not live long after the attack on his home. By 1798, Bloody Fellow had replaced Hanging Maw as principal chief.[5]

The letters and reports below were all written in the aftermath of Captain John Beard's attack on Hanging Maw's home. At the center of the storm is Daniel Smith, secretary of the Southwest Territory, the man saddled with Governor Blount's responsibilities during Blount's trip to Philadelphia. Hanging Maw is highly critical of Smith in his letter to the secretary. Regarding the attack on the Chickasaws alluded to in that letter, Hanging Maw is likely writing figuratively; the attack apparently took place in the territory overseen by Smith, not literally at Smith's home. Hanging Maw also expresses his frustrations in his letter to President George Washington.

Reports concerning the attack on Hanging Maw's house

REPORT OF MAJOR KING AND DANIEL CARMICHAEL TO SECRETARY DANIEL SMITH

Captain Chisholm's, June 12th, 1793—in the evening

Sir:

At the appearance of day light this morning, Captain John Beard, with his company of mounted infantry, to our great surprise, made an attack on the Indians at the Hanging Maw's. They have killed Scantee, Fool Charley, the Hanging Maw's wife, Betty, the daughter of Kittakiska, and we believe eight or nine others, among them William Rosebury, a white man, the Hanging Maw shot through the arm, Betty, the daughter of Nancy Ward, wounded. The fire of this inhuman party seemed to be directed at the white people who were there as much as at the Indians. Therefore, we made our escape through it as quick as possible, and cannot give a minute account of the whole of the damage. By hard pleading, we got them to spare the rest of the Hanging Maw's family, and his house from being burnt. Such a detestable act as this would be base at any time, but, as they were there at the request of Governor Blount, it will be attended with fatal consequences, and retaliation will surely take place.

We informed the white inhabitants of Baker's creek, Nine-mile, and Little river, of this horrid deed, as we came here; they are much alarmed, blame the perpetrators, expect the utmost hostility of the Indians, and are crying out for assistance on the frontiers.

Letter from Secretary Daniel Smith to Secretary of War Henry Knox

Knoxville, June 13th, 1793

Sir:

It mortifies me much that the first communications I make you, after Governor Blount's departure, should be of so disagreeable a nature. The enclosed report of Major King and Daniel Carmichael will inform you of the perpetration of as inhuman an act as ever was committed—committed by Captain John Beard, who was ordered out by Governor Blount, before his departure, to inflict punishment on the murderers of the Gilhams, and positively restricting him from crossing the Tennessee. How detestable is this act to all good men!

I shall direct Colonel White to call a court martial for the trial of Captain Beard, and mean to give the judges an attorney for the district information of his violent conduct and injuries to the Indians, that they may exert the force of law against him under the eleventh article of the Holston treaty.

I had been, for some time past, suspicious that the rage of many of the inhabitants of this district would burst out in some very unjustifiable act. But this exceeds any thing that could have been supposed.

There are many, too many, individuals of this country, whose conduct is so violent that they have no just claim to the benefits of Government, while their frenzy continues; at the same time there are great numbers of meritorious citizens who ought instantly to have it. I have written to General Sevier to exert himself quickly to execute an order issued to him by Governor Blount, to have one-third of the militia of Washington district made in readiness to march for the defence of the frontiers at an hour's notice. I did not call for them to be actually marched as yet, because a fortnight applied to labor, at this time of approaching harvest, would be highly beneficial to the inhabitants; and I must have certain information of a powerful invasion, or of its approach, before I call for them. Nor have I ordered Colonel White, of this county, to call out into actual service more than half of five of the more interior companies of militia of this county, who will be ordered to take post at the most proper places on the frontiers. I also enclose to you a copy of a letter which I addressed to the chiefs of the Cherokee nation; not that I believe my advice to them will be followed, but because I thought it my duty to make the attempt. I have directed Major King, if he believes his person could not be safe in a personal interview with any Indians he could meet near their towns, to hang up this letter in some conspicuous place, that they may be sure to get it. If it leads to any communications at all, it will be beneficial.

I regret the absence of the Governor, who, I hope, will soon be back again, for my situation is truly painful.

LETTER FROM SECRETARY SMITH TO HANGING MAW AND OTHER CHIEFS OF THE CHEROKEE NATION

Knoxville, June 13th, 1793

Friends and Brothers:

I still give you that appellation, though I confess we have not a right to have it retained. Governor Blount went away to Philadelphia, at the time he told you he would. The young inconsiderate men have taken advantage of his absence to commit the atrocious act of yesterday morning. They say, as I hear, that some Indians stole some of their horses, whom they followed as far as Coyatee. Then, foolishly supposing these Indians were some of the party at the Hanging Maw's, went there and committed the violent deed of yesterday, of which I am ashamed, and despise the perpetrators: for their act was horrid and unmanly.

I wish you to be not too angry to hear good advice. I will tell you what I think is for the good of your nation. Don't join the Creeks in the unprovoked war they are carrying on against us, but listen to the advice of Governor Blount, and go to Philadelphia, by way of Seneca, not through this country, and Mr. John M'Kee, your friend, will go with you. Be not rash and inconsiderate. Hear what your and our great father, the President, will say. Go and see him, as he has requested. I assure you, in great truth, I believe he will give you satisfaction, if you forbear to take it yourselves.

I wish you to send to me some person, who can come in safety, to let me know what you will do, and let us try if peaceful communications can take place.

LETTER FROM HANGING MAW TO PRESIDENT GEORGE WASHINGTON

Coyatee, June 15th, 1793

Beloved Father:

I received the talk of our great Father, and always held it fast. You sent me word that nothing should happen me at my own house. It was but four nights after Governor Blount left home until this happened to me.

I am writing to the President of the United States. It is a long time since I have seen him, but I have seen him, when we were both young men and warriors.

It was but a few days since I received an invitation from the President to got to Philadelphia; part of our headmen had gathered at my house, and the balance were on the way, and a party of white people came and wounded me, and killed several more, some of them chiefs. We thought very well of your talk of restoring peace, and our land being made safe to us; but the white people have spoiled the talk at present. The heads of our land thought very well of going to Philadelphia, but some of them now lie dead, and some of them wounded. You need not look for us to go there at this time. The Little Turkey has sent to the Chickasaws and Choctaws, and has gone to the Creeks himself, to let these nations know that he was going to Philadelphia this Fall, that a head-man from each nation might accompany him, that the whole might agree on one thing, and all be at peace.

LETTER FROM HANGING MAW TO SECRETARY DANIEL SMITH

Coyatee, June 15th, 1793

Friend and Brother:

It is but a few days since you were left in the place of Governor Blount. While he was in place, nothing happened.

Surely they are making their fun of you. Surely you are no head-man nor warrior. I am just informed you will take satisfaction for me, and I shall reckon it just the same as if I had taken it myself. I reckon you are afraid of these thieves, when you talk of sending to Congress. If you are left in the place of Governor, you ought to take satisfaction yourself. It was but a few days since I was at your house, and you told me that nothing should happen to me nor any people at my house; but since that, blood has been spilt at both our houses. I reckon that the white people are just making their fun of you. Governor Blount always told me that nothing should happen me as long as I did live, but he had hardly got out of sight until I was invaded by them, and like to have got killed. I think you are afraid of these bad men. They first killed the Chickasaws at your house, and this is the second time of their doing mischief. I think you are afraid of them. When is the day that a white man was killed at my house? I think the white men make fun of you. Now, blood is spilt at both of our houses by your people. I think they are making fun of you, and won't listen to your talks.

LETTER FROM SECRETARY DANIEL SMITH TO DOUBLEHEAD

Knoxville, June 17, 1793

Friend and Brother:

I am in much sorrow and trouble on account of the blood

which has lately been shed in your land in so disgraceful a manner. I want to redress your wrongs, and doubt not of doing it, if you forbear to take satisfaction yourselves. The Hanging Maw has written to our beloved father the President. I will have his letter conveyed, with one which I will write myself, to him and Governor Blount. I beg you to wait till you hear from them. The innocent ought not to die for the guilty, which would be the case if you take satisfaction yourselves. The President has waited long, and forborne to take satisfaction of those who have killed and robbed his people, because he knows the innocent would then be punished with the guilty, which would make him sorry. You know it was agreed, in the treaty at this place, that if any white men of the United States should go into your land and commit crimes there, against your people, they shall be punished for it in the same manner as if the crime had been committed against white people. You know that it was also agreed that, in case of violence being committed on the personal property of the individuals of either party, neither retaliation nor reprisal should be made by the other, until satisfaction should have been demanded of the offending party, and *refused*.

The President is a great and good man, and will keep his word, and I beg of you not to take satisfaction yourselves, but wait, and let us punish them for you. Thus may peace be restored to the land.

LETTER FROM JOHN THOMPSON
TO SECRETARY DANIEL SMITH

Hanging Maw's, 18th June, 1793

Sir:

I came here yesterday from the Little Turkey, with the letter to Governor Blount by me. But hearing that a man could not pass through the settlements with safety, I concluded to stay where I was. I send Mr. Fulton on with the letter, and I refer you to him for the news in this land, and likewise the Creeks, and among the Spaniards. He can give you the full accounts of all that's passing. You will see what the Turkey has to say. There are about forty or fifty Indians here, come to see the Hanging Maw, and others that were wounded, and provision is hard to be got, without you send orders or appoint a man to get it for them. There are a good many gone back that were coming to trade and pay what debts they owed to the people in the settlements. The Indians are for peace, if the whites will let them alone. They say it is best to leave it to the consideration of their brothers of the United States, and see what will be done for them. They have sent runners through the whole nation, not for a man to attempt to take satisfaction, until they see what is to be done. I am starving myself. I have spoken to Mr. Fulton to speak for some flour and some dried meat, for my own use, as I expect to stay here some time. I will be much obliged to you, if you will be so good as to assist him; and I have sent for the other articles, such as goods, to be brought out to buy;

there are furs here. There is no danger for a person to come out to this place.

The Indians intend to send you their talks; there are about ten or twelve head-men at this place.

LETTER FROM SECRETARY DANIEL SMITH TO SECRETARY OF WAR HENRY KNOX

Knoxville, June 22d, 1793

Sir:

Since writing you on the 17th instant, other communications have taken place with the Cherokees. The enclosed papers, which I have the honor to transmit, will shew what they have been, as nothing material is left out of them.

You will observe the Indians have agreed to wait and hear the determination of the President. The nation, because of scarcity of provision, and attention to their crops, is not [in] a condition for a general war, and I believe the chiefs are sincere; but I doubt their power to influence all small parties to pacific measures. It seems to me, that without some unexpected and unforeseen event diverts their attention, powerful invasions from them will ensue; I mean after sufficient time elapses to transmit your answer. The animosity from the whites continues as high against them as ever, as the Indians have lately stolen horses from Gamble's station, and, to my great pain, I find, to punish Beard by law, just now, is out of the question.

I have thought it expedient to order a subaltern's command of horse from Capt. Evans' company, not more than eight or nine, for a short time, to commence next week, to reconnoiter the woods for about twenty miles westward of Southwest Point, to discover the approach of an enemy, for within that bounds they will be most likely to direct that course to attack the northwest frontier. And I shall also use all means in my power to draw information from the nation.

I at first thought of writing you by post, but on reconsidering the matter, believe it best to send express, to prevent accidental delays.

After writing the foregoing, as I was closing the letter, Colonel Doherty arrived here, and brings me certain information of a large party of Indians being in Wear's Cove, on Little Pigeon; they have cut down about a quarter of an acre of corn, killed one horse, stolen ten others, took seven bags of meal out of Wear's mill, and broke to pieces such parts of the mill as they could, with little difficulty; also killed two cows and one hog. This was done on the night of the 19th instant; I have only to remark, that this mischief too quickly succeeded the unwarrantable action at the Hanging Maw's, to have been occasioned by it; and there is the strongest reason to believe the perpetrators came from the town of Tallassee, or another town above it. Colonel Doherty tells me Lieutenant Henderson, who is in service with about thirty men, was yesterday to set out in pursuit of the enemy. I have not yet determined what further order to take on the occasion, but I shall restrict the whites to defensive measures only.[6]

Letter from Secretary Daniel Smith to Captain John Beard

July 17th, 1793

Sir:

As the court martial has not yet proceeded to judgment on your former conduct, you are yet to be considered as an officer subject to the order of Government, and I now call upon you, requiring you to desist from your unwarantable conduct, to disband your men, and send them to their respective homes. It must be expected that all officers will pay regard to these orders, which I require you to make known to them; their oaths cannot be so lightly looked upon, or, at least, I hope they are not, as to permit them to disregard this order, for they will have to answer the contrary at their peril.[7]

ACCORDING TO THE LAW OF
THIS COUNTRY, 1801-02

◆➤◀◆➤◀◆➤◀◆➤◀◆➤◀◆➤◀◆➤◀◆➤◀◆➤◀◆➤◀◆➤◀◆➤◀◆➤◀

Return Jonathan Meigs was born in Middletown, Connecticut, in 1740. He served as a lieutenant in the Sixth Connecticut Regiment and was promoted to the rank of colonel during the Revolutionary War. In May 1801, the Jefferson administration appointed him special agent to the Cherokees. Meigs also accepted a dual appointment as an agent of the United States War Department for Tennessee.[1]

He arrived in Cherokee country in June 1801 and immediately began establishing a combined Indian and War Department agency at South West Point in what is now Kingston, Tennessee. Meigs also established a secondary agency at Tellico at the request of several prominent Cherokees, including James Vann.

As agent to the Cherokees, Meigs had many duties,

including distributing farm and household implements, investigating and removing intruders from Cherokee lands, and promoting the transition from a hunting to an agricultural economy. He encouraged the Cherokees to establish a republican government and served as mediator between them and state and local governments.[2]

Meigs faced pressure from the national and state governments to obtain land cessions from the Cherokees. During negotiations, Meigs argued that the money and goods the Cherokees would receive for their lands were more valuable than the lands themselves. However, he also had a reputation for standing up for Indian rights during the treaty conferences and for obtaining fair monetary settlements for land cessions and injustices done to the Cherokees.

In January 1823, the eighty-two-year-old Meigs gave up his warm bed to an aged Cherokee leader. As a result of sleeping on the cold floor, Meigs developed pneumonia and later died. He had served as Cherokee agent for twenty-two years.[3]

James Vann was a mixed-blood Cherokee, the grandson of a Scotsman and a Cherokee woman named Ruth Gamn. Born in 1768 at Spring Place, Georgia, Vann built a large brick house on his family's plantation, Diamond Hill. He owned many slaves and a ferry on the Chattahoochee River.[4] Vann was instrumental in helping the Moravians establish a mission station at Spring Place in 1801.[5]

In 1803, Vann aided Meigs in obtaining permission from the Cherokee Council to build a road running north and south through the Cherokee country. Branches from the Hiwassee River and Nashville would connect near Spring Hill in Georgia. Vann built a store and public house along the new road at Spring Place.[6]

Vann had a reputation for drinking and carousing. Although he was helpful to Meigs in some of his dealings with the Cherokees, he was also a thorn in Meigs's side. Meigs received reports that Vann had murdered a Georgia militiaman named Leonard Rice. In 1804, Meigs sent a list of Vann's misdeeds to the secretary of war.[7] In 1809, Vann was ambushed and shot to death as he left a tavern.[8]

Meigs recorded correspondence on various incidents in his Cherokee agency daybook. The excerpts below are taken from that daybook. The first two concern the search for justice following the murder of a Cherokee woman. The matter is of such concern to the United States that President Thomas Jefferson and his secretary of state, soon-to-be president James Madison, issued a proclamation and a reward for the capture of the perpetrators. The bulk of the excerpts concern Vann's appeals to Meigs for assistance in obtaining the release of a Cherokee who has been arrested for stealing a horse. In two letters regarding that incident, Meigs raises the point that Indians are not allowed to testify in courts. The correspondence between Meigs and Judge McNairy alludes to a separate horse-stealing incident, in which a Mr. T. Macklin has taken a horse from the son of Little Turkey and is obliged to make good with a horse of equal value.

Unfortunately, there are no more entries in the daybook for 1802, and there is no mention of the outcome of the search for the killer of the Cherokee woman or the arrest of the Cherokee for the stolen horse.

Excerpts from the daybook of Return J. Meigs

LETTER FROM SECRETARY OF WAR
HENRY DEARBORN TO RETURN J. MEIGS

War Department 2d Dec. 1801

Sir—

You will herewith receive a copy of the Presidents proclamation offering a reward for apprehending the persons who lately murdered a Cherokee Woman, and request you as soon as possible to have it published in the Tennessee paper, and copies of it stuck up at public places, and use your best endeavours to have its contents explained through out the Cherokee Nation— [9]

BY THE PRESIDENT OF THE
UNITED STATES OF AMERICA
A PROCLAMATION

Whereas information has been received That an atrocious Murder was in the Month of August last committed on an

Indian Woman of the Cherokee Tribe in the peace and friendship of the United States, in the County of Knox in the state of Tennessee, aggravated also by the consideration that it was committed at a moment when a friendly meeting was about to be held by Commissioners of the United States, with the Chiefs of the said Tribe of Indians, for the purpose of making certain arrangements favourable to the tranquility and advantage of the frontier settlers, as well as just and eligible to the Indians themselves. And whereas the apprehension and punishment of the Murderers and their accessaries will be an example due to justice and humanity, and every way salutory in its apperation: I have therefore thought fit to issue this my proclamation hereby exhorting the Citizens of the United States, and requiring all the officers thereof according to their respective stations, to use their utmost endeavors to apprehend and bring the principals and accessaries to the said Murder to Justice. And I do moreover offer a reward of one thousand Dollars for each principal, and five hundred Dollars for each accessary to the crime before the fact, who shall be apprehended and brought to Justice.

In testimony whereof, I have caused the seal of the United States of America, to be affixed to these presents and signed, the same with my hand. Done at the City of Washington, the thirtieth Day of November in the year of our Lord one thousand eight hundred and one, and of the Independence of the United States of America the twenty sixth.

Thos. Jefferson
James Madison, Secy of State[10]

LETTER FROM JAMES VANN TO RETURN J. MEIGS

Diamond Hill 28th Decr. 1801

Sir—

Two Indians arrived at my House this day, and informed me that at their Camps on the waters of Caney fork in Cumberlan a Creek Indian came to their camp with a Horse— and requested one of the Cherokees to accompany him to a house 7 or 8 miles from the camp for the purpose of assisting him in selling his horse for Whiskey—the Cherokee consented and rode the horse the Creek followed on behind on foot and when coming in sight of the house the Creek declined going any farther—the Cherokee with the horse went to the house and stayed all Night—purchased some whiskey in the morning and started for his Camp again—when he [was] pursued by eight white men, the Creek fellow had got back to the Camp sometime before the young man that rode his Horse and when the Whites came into the Camp he was out in the woods a small distance Cuting Saddle trees to make himself a Sadle he saw the white people when coming to the Cherokee Camp—and fled and was not seen afterwards— leaving behind him at the Camp a very fine Rifle Gun—The white immediately seized the Cherokee that stayed at the house all Night with the horse, and carried him off prisoner, and took the Creeks Gun and his own—This is the account the Indians gave me that have come in and they wish you to make enquiry respecting the matter, and rectify the mistake that their companion may be relieved— [11]

LETTER FROM RETURN J. MEIGS
TO JUDGE MCNAIRY

South West Point
1st Jany 1802

Sir—

I have been informed that a Cherokee Indian has been
commited to jail in Nashville for stealing a Horse from a Citi-
zen of Cumberland—I do not wish to extenuate the Crime if
it is possible to get over this affair with out great rigor. I should
be glad, the Indians are very apt to charge us with partiality
in matters relating breaches of Law where they are con-
cerned— They are still complaining of the murder of the Indian woman and for want of knowledge of the order of our
Laws, are apt to consider our prudent proceedings as der-
eliction of Justice—

I once spoke to you, Sir, about Mr. T. Macklin taking a
Horse from the Little Turkeys son, and have been since obliged
to pay for the Horse to the Little Turkey. Have wrote to Mr.
Macklin, but have received no answer—as you have been
applyed to on this matter by the former Agent and know the
circumstance—Permit me, Sir, to request you to speak once
more to him, Macklin on the Subject—I am unwilling from
the circumstances to commence an action—

Mr. Maclin is certainly exposed to the penalty of the Law—But if he will pay the price which the Law has fixed for Horses in such cases, I shall not commence an action against him, otherwise I shall do it—

P.S. Since writing the above I have received a letter from James Vann a Copy of which I enclose to you—The statement made by him from the Indians appears to be true—It seems that the Creek Indian deceived and imposed on the Cherokee to sell the Horse, in order to screen himself—& his making his escape when the whites appeared confirms in my mind, that the Creek and not the Cherokee is the person who stole the Horse— [12]

LETTER FROM JUDGE MCNAIRY TO RETURN J. MEIGS

Belloein 7th Jany 1802

Sir.

Yours dated the first Instant enclosing a Copy of the letter from Mr. James Vann was received by yesterdays Mail. The Indian you mention is confined in Nashville Goal [jail], under State authority. I have taken some steps by which I suppose, he will be transferred to the Federal Court—If the matter should come before the Court by presentment or In-

dictment, it is obliged to go off as the facts may appear then—
But I am inclined to believe, that affidavits regularly taken by
you and transmitted to the attorney for the United States in
the District of West Tennessee, would indue him by consent
of the Court, to enter Nolli poseque [nolle prosequi, a court
entry made when a prosecutor will proceed no farther in an
action], especially if they go to establish the facts mentioned
in Vanns letter. If this is not done, it will be necessary that the
Indians and others who may be witnesses for the prisoner
should attend the Circuit Court to be held on the 20th of
April next at Nashville. If all this should fail to aquit the Indian, I have no doubt but that the President upon application
by fit characters, having also a true representation of the case,
would pardon him—Acting as a private individual I think
precicely with you and suppose it good policy, not to deal
rigourously with him. Since I saw you have spoken to Maclin
about the Horse, he expresses his willingness to pay the Little
Turkeys son a horse equal to the one he received, and pay for
some other articles the Indians complained about. What he
will say about paying Money for the Horse, I don't know, but
will speak to him upon sight, he is well aware, that he is liable to the penalty—If some person here was authorized to
receive from him, it might sooner yet.[13]

LETTER FROM RETURN J. MEIGS TO JAMES VANN

South West Point—28th Jany 1802

Sir.

I have received your letter of the 28th December last, Stating the circumstances that took place in the Indian Camp on Caney fork in Cumberland, from which a Cherokee man was taken and sent to Nashville Goal, being charged with Stealing a Horse—I sent a Copy of your letter to Judge McNary at Nashville requesting him to consider the case in the Most favorable light as it respects the Indian who is confined—

The Judge advises that regular Depositions be taken of the affair from any person who may know anything of the transactions—

I wish to have depositions taken from the Indians who were present of at least two of them—

If no Magistrate can be found convenient—I wish you to take the depositions yourself and after the Indians have Signed them with their marks—to have them witnessed by two White men—and then that you sign them at the Bottom with your name as a Cherokee Chief—I have sent the form of a Deposition in which you will observe I have inserted the substance of your letter to me—this is only a form—if the Indians can testify anything more it will of course be in the Deposition which you take—I am sensible that the Law knows nothing of the Evidence of Indians, but I am of opinion that it will be of use—and it is to be wished that the Indians may comprehend the nature of an Oath—If you cannot get the Depositions, the Indians who are knowing to the affair must attend at the trial on the 20th of April next at Nashville—Judge McNary appears disposed to consider the affair in as favorable a manner as possible. I don't know the names of the Indians & have put fictitious names in the form of a Deposition which I have sent you—You must put the real names in when you take their depositions—the sooner the business is done the better— [14]

DEPOSITION FORM SENT BY RETURN J. MEIGS TO JAMES VANN

Personally appeared before me James Vann a Cherokee Chief John True and George Right and being Solemnly called on by me to speak the truth in the presence of the Great Spirit Deposed as follows viz: That being in their camp on the waters of Caney Fork in Cumberland on or about the ___ day of December 1801 A Creek Indian came to their Camp with a Horse and requested one of the Cherokees to accompany him to a House seven or Eight miles from the Camp for the purpose of assisting him in selling his Horse for Whiskey—The Cherokee consented and rode the Horse, the Creek Indian followed on behind on foot and when coming in sight of the House, the Creek declined going any further, the Cherokee (with the Horse) went to the House and stayed all night purchased some whiskey in the morning and started for his

Camp again—when he was pursued by eight White men—
The Creek Indian had got back to the Camp before the Cherokee man who rode his horse and when the White men came
to the Camp the Creek man was out in the Woods a small
distance Cutting Saddle trees to make himself a Saddle—He
saw the White people coming to the Camp and fled, and was
not seen afterwards, leaving behind him at the Camp a very
fine Rifle Gun—The White men immediately seized the
Cherokee who had stayed at the House all Night with the
Horse and carried him off a prisoner, and took the Creeks
Gun and his own—

Witnesses present

The above deposition Was taken before me on
The __ Day of __
A.D. 1802
James Vann, a Cherokee Chief[15]

Letter from Return J. Meigs to Judge McNairy

South West point—10th Feby 1802

Sir.

I have been honored with your letter of the 17th Ulto.

[ultimo—i.e., of the preceding month] since I received it, I have wrote to James Vann requesting him to obtain depositions of Indians or others stating the circumstances that took place relative to and previous to the confinement of the Indian who is now in Nashville Goal & desired Mr. Vann (provided he could not get the Depositions) to send forward those Indians who were at the Indian Camp at the time the Indian was taken, to attend the trial on the 20th April next I have not received his answer to my letter—

But have this day recd a second letter from Mr. Vann of which I enclose you a Copy—By which you will observe that the affair has much Interested the Indians in behalf of the person—they urge me to use my interest to have him removed to this place, that he may be tried by his Countrymen, by his peers—You, Sir, will Judge of the legality, and the propriety, or the reasonableness, or the policy of such a step—If the Indian was taken by legal process within the bounds of Tennessee, I presume the request cannot be complained with. But if he was taken without regular legal Steps and within the Indian boundary, on lands which are by treaty granted to the Indians and which I have understood to be the case ought he not to be given up agreeably to the request of the Chiefs. But if he must be brought to trial at Nashville—I have no doubt of the Courts assigning him able Counsel—The people are in a State of nature—emerging slowly from barbarism towards civilization—they are under the protection of the United States: but we legislate and we execute, we treat them as free Agence in some respects, and in them as mere Infants—they cannot be witnesses in Law sense—Yet can suffer as free moral Agents—this situation is a pitiful one—I do not make these remarks as reflections on our Legislators or Judiciary—in my heart I honor them but in considering the case of these helpless beings, I think their disabilities will certainly plead for them, and seem to say, do not hurt me for I cannot Defend myself— [16]

LETTER FROM JAMES VANN
AND OTHER CHEROKEES TO RETURN J. MEIGS

Cherokee Nation—5th Feby 1802

Sir—

We the hed men from Oostenaley, Rabbittrap, Criswattee, had a talk concerning the Indian fellow which is confined in Cumberland, and had him there this long time, and we are desirous that he should be sent to you, as you are the Agent to our Nation from the United States, and we will send some of our head men to the West point, and if he has done any thing amiss he may have a trial at the West point and shall have his punishment according to the Law of this Country, hoping that you will get him as soon as possible, and keep him in confinement untill some of our head men will be there with you. [17]

An Ardent Zeal, 1818

✦⬩◀✦⬩◀✦⬩◀✦⬩◀✦⬩◀✦⬩◀✦⬩◀✦⬩◀✦⬩◀✦⬩◀✦⬩◀✦⬩◀✦⬩◀✦⬩◀✦⬩◀

The Chickamaugah Mission to the Cherokees—named after the creek in southeastern Tennessee where it was located — opened its doors in 1817. It was renamed in 1818 for David Brainerd, a missionary who had worked among the Northern Indians many years earlier. Brainerd was not the first mission to the Cherokees. The Moravian Mission at Spring Place, Georgia, had opened its doors in 1802, and the Reverend Gideon Blackburn had established a school that closed its doors in 1810. Other missions to the Cherokees in the early nineteenth century included Creek Path and Will's Town in Alabama; Haweis, Hightower, Carmel, and Oothcaloga in Georgia; and Runningwater Town, Red Clay, and Candy's Creek in Tennessee.

One of the most important visitors to Brainerd Mission was President James Monroe, who called there in May 1819. Between 1835 and 1838, the missionaries opened the doors to Cherokees who had been forced out of their homes in Georgia. They held services at the Red Clay council grounds for Cherokees who gathered there to discuss the impending Removal to the Arkansas Territory and how they could fight it. The doors closed on the Brainerd Mission in September 1838, as several teachers and missionaries prepared to accompany the Cherokees to the West.[1]

The first excerpt below—the report of a three-man commission to the American Board of Commissioners for Foreign Missions—gives an overview of the early days of the Brainerd Mission. It touches on the facilities, the staff, expenditures, the student body, and the curriculum, particularly Christian instruction and its effect on Cherokee students.

The second excerpt is a letter from a former student, Catharine Brown, who finds herself missing the Brainerd Mission very much.

Catharine was born near Will's Town in what is now DeKalb County, Alabama, around 1800. In July 1817, she enrolled in the newly established Brainerd, where she was baptized in January 1818. Her brother A-wih, or David Brown, enrolled at Brainerd in 1819 and became one of the school's premier scholars. He, a Cherokee student named John Arch, and the Reverend Daniel S. Butrick created a Cherokee spelling book. In September 1825, David completed the translation of the New Testament directly from a Greek text to the Cherokee alphabet.

In January 1818, Catharine's parents removed her from

Brainerd in preparation for a move west to the Arkansas Territory, where many other Cherokee families had already settled. The move was delayed, and Catharine returned to her beloved friends at the Brainerd Mission. In December 1818, Catharine was again withdrawn from the Brainerd school. After a tearful farewell to her missionary friends, she left with her parents for the West. It was early in this second absence when she composed the letter included in this chapter. In May 1819, her father brought her back to Brainerd.

When the Cherokee mission schools at Brainerd and Spring Place became overcrowded, the Cherokees of Creek Path in Will's Valley petitioned the American Board of Commissioners for Foreign Missions to establish a new school at Creek Path. Catharine Brown was recommended to teach at the school. Not long after her arrival at the Creek Path school, both Catharine and her brother John became ill. John died in January 1822 and Catharine in 1823.[2]

Flora Chamberlain, to whom Catharine's letter is addressed, was the daughter of Brainerd missionary Ard Hoyt. She married William Chamberlain, a young missionary from Pennsylvania, on March 22, 1818, less than two weeks after his arrival at Brainerd. The roles of Flora and William Chamberlain at Brainerd are discussed in the report of the three-man commission included here. The Chamberlains remained at Brainerd until 1824, when they moved to the Will's Town Mission in Alabama. They left Will's Town in 1838, when it and many other Cherokee missions were closed due to the Removal.[3]

Report on the Brainerd Mission to the American Board of Commissioners for Foreign Missions, by Isaac Anderson, Matthew Donald, and David Campbell

Brainerd, On Chickamaugah, Cherokee Nation, May 29th [1818]

Having been, by you, appointed a visiting committee for this school, for the purpose of examining its general state and management, expenditures and improvements, we met agreeably to a previous appointment, and after the most careful examination agreed to the following report.—

The Missionaries for this Establishment have commenced the work with enlarged and liberal views. In the accommodations for the school and those connected with it, they have laid a foundation for extensive and growing usefulness. There is a large house, judiciously constructed and nearly finished, for the reception of the missionaries and their families, in which they now reside; a large dining room connected with a Kitchen; a number of cabins for lodging the girls and boys apart; with several other necessary out houses, such as meat houses, corn houses, stables, &c. There is a large schoolhouse constructed on the Lancastrian plan [a system used in many charity-sponsored schools where older students taught the younger ones]; close & warm and nearly finished, which will contain 100 Scholars. The whole establishment is on a beautiful site near a large creek called Chickamaugah which has some good bottom land. The adjacent high land is generally thin but affords excellent summer range, and a considerable quantity of it is fit for agriculture. We suppose there may be between 40 and 50 acres of cleared land enclosed by good fences and under cultivation.

There is also a grist mill in a state of feswardness [deterioration], belonging to the institution which must be of essential service. Likewise, a considerable quantity of live stock: 7 horses, a yoke of oxen, 13 siers [sires, adult male bovines or possibly stallions], 19 cows, 17 yearlings, 10 calves, 40 sheep, 40 hogs, and sixty pigs. The procuring of this stock we consider as a wise and economical regulation and must be of peculiar service to the institution, both by affording a supply of the necessaries of life, and by saving great expenses to the society.

In the management of this missionary station and its concerns, there has been a judicious distribution of the business into several departments. The Rev. Ard Hoyt has the general superintendence and oversight of the whole missionary establishment with the pastoral charge of the church. Mr. Moody Hall takes the management of all pecuniary matters, makes the necessary purchases, keeps the books, and has the oversight of the plantations, stock, &c.

The Rev. William Chamberlain has the charge of the school as instructor, and takes the direction of the boys out of school, assigns to each their employment, and labors with them for the sake of the example, as well as to direct and encourage them. Mrs. Chamberlain takes the direction of the female scholars out of school and instructs them in sewing, spinning, knitting, and the various things relating to house keeping. The Rev. Daniel S. Butrick is acquiring a knowledge of the language of the natives, investigating its grammatical construction, and laboring as an evangelist.

On the subject of expenditures, we can say that the expenses must necessarily have been great when we take into view the various buildings connected with the institution: dwelling house, school house, mill, lumber house, and many other out houses which are indispensably necessary. To this must be added the purchase of the improvements of the plantation, the expense of the repairs which have been made, the purchase of the live stock, horses, cattle, sheep, & hogs, and also the purchase of kitchen furniture for the use of the missionary families and the whole school. The expenses of provisions must have been considerable for so large a number, which was necessarily brought a great distance, and last season were both scarce & dear. But there is reason to believe that the annual expenses hereafter, will not be as great, while the school remains at this place, as they have been. The proceeds of the farm and stock will go far towards furnishing the provisions for the institution. The expenses of building, purchasing stock, &c., will not again recur, so that their two heavy expenses will not be felt again by the Society. Mr. Hall exhibited to us the accounts which set forth the whole debts and credits, and appears to have been fairly and properly kept.

There has been in this school, as we have been informed, 78 Scholars in all who have progressed less or more in learning to speak the English language, to read and write. There are at present 48 Scholars in the school, 15 of whom can read the Bible with ease & propriety. 11 others can read in easy lessons. 20 are spelling in words of one or two syllables, 2 are learning the alphabet, 4 have commenced the English grammar, all writing, except the two who are at the alphabet. Some of them write a fair legible hand and all write well for the time they have been in the school. The proficiency of these scholars in sacred music delighted us much. The order, docility, cheerfulness, and obedience of the pupils and all the regulations respecting the school were truly pleasing. The regularity by which they are disposed of out of school to the several employments assigned them. Their promptitude to obey, and dispatch to execute [in] regard to any thing of the kind we have seen. June 1st, [the] tour committee tarried at the missionary's station until after the Sabbath, that we might have an opportunity of observing the moral and religious influence which this institution has had on the scholars and neighborhood. On the Lord's day the sacrament of the Supper was administered a congregation something over one hundred collect of Cherokees, Africans, and some whites. During divine service the people were composed, very attentive; many of them solemn and some tender. Five of the natives joined in communion: one of them a young female aged about 18, a member of the school, the others live in the neighborhood. Two blacks also joined, one of them a freed man, the other a female slave. We conversed particularly with most of them on their knowledge of the gospel and their experimental acquaintance with religion. We were truly pleased with the scriptural and feeling account they gave of Christ formed in them; the hope of Glory. We had similar conversation with several others who had not yet been united to the church that gave good evidence of a saving change of heart, particularly with two Indians and two white men connected with Indian families. These four would be readily admitted into churches where less caution was necessary than in an infant church in a heathen land. One of these was a very old Indian woman who could not speak English, but could understand what was said to her and had to answer us by an interpreter.

She lamented that she had not heard the word of God when young, but said since she had heard it, she had tried to do good. Her knowledge of divine subjects was really surprising. She was much affected during divine service. One who had joined the church said he had been made to see himself a vile sinner; that when walking about in deep distress he felt he was not worthy to walk on the earth. All with whom we conversed expressed a deep sense of their sinfulness and guilt and of their need of a Savior. One said when she was under conviction she was tempted to think that there was nothing in religion, at least that Indians would get to heaven without it, and that Christianity was necessary for white people only. She said she was afraid to begin to pray lest she might not continue, but her distress became so great she had to cry to God for mercy. This young beautiful creature is now an ornament of religion and in and of her sex. When she felt she had embraced the Savior, before she was admitted to the church and even without its having been suggested to her, she had the courage and zeal to read, sing, and pray morning and evening in the girls' house with her female school mates to encourage and exhort them to pray. When she first came to the school, we were informed, she was proud & haughty, loaded with yearnings & Jewels. She is now modest and humble, has stripped off the greatest part of jewels, and consecrated them to the Society for Foreign Missions as did another of the natives. Since she joined the church, this young female is now an active member of a praying female society. Would not the conduct of many mothers in Israel blush before the example and zeal of this girl? Is not the Lord raising her up and qualifying her for a missionary? For this work she has an ardent zeal.

There are some others under religious impressions with whom we had no opportunity of conversation. Numbers of the congregation came 10, 15, and 20 Miles to be at church. We were told, that in taking a walk morning or evening, little girls from 8 to 12 years of age may be heard praying [in] secret places and we observed several of them very serious and attentive to divine things.

From what we have seen in this school and neighborhood, we are convinced that the direct way to civilize a heathen people is to Christianize them. After public worship, we waited to inspect the Sabbath School taught by Mr. Hall. The scholars were blacks and we were informed had been sometime as many as 30 in number. 14 of this school have in one year learned to read in the testament, the rest are spelling. They were attentive, serious, and anxious for religious instruction. One of them belongs to the church. Two others have been examined and propounded for admission. Of two others, hopes are entertained. The young female spoken of above voluntarily offered to assist in teaching the blacks and is now engaged in the benevolent work. A native who has now joined the church, mistress of one of the blacks, but who cannot read, is learning from her slave who is taught in this Sunday school.

Surely the Lord is in this place. The work is His and it is marvelous in our eyes. Will not Christians be encouraged to pray for it's prosperity? Will they not cheerfully support it by their liberality? To meet one of their souls in heaven, rescued from hell, eternal gloom, by the instrumentality of Christianity exertion? O, what unspeakable joy! The Lord may rescue hundreds of them speedily. The present appearances are encouraging.[4]

LETTER FROM CATHARINE BROWN
TO WILLIAM AND FLORA CHAMBERLAIN
AT THE BRAINERD MISSION

Fort Deposit December the 12th [1818]

I jest sit down to address you with my pen, but is this all? Am I so soon called to bid you adieux and see your faces no more in this world? O, my beloved friends. You know not the love I bear to that blessed spot where I have spent so many happy hours with you, dear friends. I weep, my heart is full, but it is past, never to return. Tears flow from my eyes while I write; and why is it so, do I murmur? God forbid. Ought I not to praise the Lord for what I have received, and trust him for every thing? O, yes, His ways are best and He has graciously promised that all things shall work together for good to those that love Him. But do I love Him? Have I that love to Him that will enable me to keep all His commandments? Do I love Him with all my heart? O, that the Lord would search me and lead me in the way of eternal life.

Since I left you, [I am] leading a very lonesome life and not hearing the gospel preached but once. That is when Father Hoyt was here and maybe they came here on Tuesday evening. I was sitting in my room, I heared a knocking at the door, I bid them come in and who but brother Mylo [Hoyt] appeared. I inquired if any body was with him. He said his father was at the door. That rejoiced me very much and I enjoyed very much while they was here. Blessed be God for sending them here to instruct us. I am here amongst a wicked set of people and never hear prayers nor any Godly conversation. O, my dear friends, pray for me. I hope you do. There is not a day passes but I think of you and the kindness I received during the time I stayed with you. It is not my wish to go to the Arkansas but God only knows what is best for me. I shall not attempt to tell you what I have felt since I left you and the tears I have shed when I called to mind the happy moments we passed in singing the praises of God. However, I bear it as well as I possibly can; trusting in our dear Savior who will never leave nor forsake them that puts their trust in him. It may be possible that I may see you once more. It would be a great happiness to me if I don't go to the Arkansas. Perhaps I may, but if I should go it is not likely we shall meet in this world again. But you will excuse me, for my heart feels that which I cannot express with my pen. When I think and see the poor thoughtless Cherokees going on in sin I can not help blessing God that has lead me in the right path to serve Him. Father will start to the Arkansas about some time after Christmas but I am not certain that I shall go.

I thank you for your kind letters. Do write to me every opportunity, I shall conclude w[ith] my love to all my brothers and sisters at Brainerd. Sister Flora, do kiss all the children for me. I shall expect letters from all the little girls. O, may we all meet at last in the kingdom of our blessed Savior, never more to part. Farewell my dear brother and sister. Farewell.[5]

To Rise from
Their Ashes, 1828-31

In 1821, Sequoyah, or George Gist, presented his new Cherokee syllabary to Cherokee leaders. Based on the phonetic sounds
in the Cherokee language, his syllabary consisted of eighty-six
symbols, representing six vowels and eighty consonants and con-
sonant-vowel combinations. Within a short period, thousands of
Cherokees were able to read and write their language.[1]

In 1825, with literacy in the Cherokee Nation growing rapidly, the Cherokee National Council authorized Elias Boudinot
to travel the country to solicit donations for a printing press and
a national academy. Boudinot gave speeches in New York, Bos-
ton, Philadelphia, Charleston, and other large cities.[2]

Boudinot was born Killakeena, or Buck Watie, and was the

son of Major Ridge's brother, Oowatie. Buck Watie changed his name to Elias Boudinot after meeting the distinguished patriot and philanthropist of that name.[3]

In October 1827, Elias Boudinot's prospectus for the *Cherokee Phoenix* was published. It was republished in the second issue of the *Cherokee Phoenix* on February 28, 1828.[4] Early that year, the press, type, and furniture for the printing office arrived in New Echota. The Cherokee Council hired a white printer, Isaac Harris, at a salary of four hundred dollars per year. Boudinot was allotted three hundred dollars per year as editor, translator, office manager, and apprentice to Harris. The American Board of Commissioners for Foreign Missions supplemented Boudinot's salary with an additional one hundred dollars per year to make it equitable with the salary of the white printer.

The first issue of the *Cherokee Phoenix* was published on February 21, 1828. A year later, the name was changed to the *Cherokee Phoenix and Indian's Advocate*.[5] It was a weekly paper printed in both English and Cherokee, but due to problems in obtaining supplies, it was not always published on the same day of the week and was sometimes delayed for more than a week. The newspaper was widely circulated in the United States and Europe.[6] The translation of articles into the Cherokee language was, according to Boudinot, "by far the most arduous part of our labor."[7] As a result, only selected articles and reports—such as Cherokee laws, political notices, and scriptures—were translated into the Cherokee syllabary.

In 1832, Boudinot began to favor the idea of removal to the

West. He felt the Cherokee people had a right to read arguments on both sides of the issue and wanted to publish his views in favor of removal. The Cherokee government prohibited him from doing that. Due to this censorship and pressure from Cherokee leader John Ross, Boudinot resigned as editor in August 1832. John Ross's brother-in-law, Elijah Hicks, was chosen to replace him.[8]

In 1835, John Ross planned to move the printing press of the *Cherokee Phoenix* to Red Clay for protection from the Georgia Guard. However, minutes before his wagon arrived at Elijah Hicks's house to pick up the press, Stand Watie (Boudinot's brother) and the Georgia Guard confiscated the press, type, paper, and books. The fate of the press is not known, but it was allegedly used in Cassville, Georgia, to print notices calling Cherokees to attend the meeting that would result in the 1835 Treaty of New Echota, the so-called Removal Treaty.[9] John Ridge, Major Ridge, Elias Boudinot, Stand Watie, and John Adair Bell, a friend of Ridge's and son of a prominent Cherokee family, were all signers of the Treaty of New Echota.[10]

On June 22, 1839, Major Ridge, John Ridge, and Elias Boudinot were murdered near their homes in the Arkansas Territory. Stand Watie and John Adair Bell narrowly escaped the same fate when they were warned by messenger of the deaths of the Ridges and Boudinot.[11] The murders were partly in retaliation for the roles the men had played in the treaty and the 1838 Removal. Although John Ross was initially suspected of having ordered the murders, participants in the killings later cleared him of any involvement.[12]

Below are excerpts from the *Cherokee Phoenix*. The selection includes the prospectus for the creation of the newspaper, a notice of candidates for office, news items, letters from readers who wish to honor a recently deceased woman or to commemorate the principal chiefs of the Cherokees, and an Elias Boudinot editorial on Indian clans. John Ridge, the author of the obituary for OO-DAH-YEE, was the well-educated son of Major Ridge, speaker of the Cherokee National Council. In 1830, John Ridge was elected president of the National Committee.[13]

Excerpts from the Cherokee Phoenix

"PROSPECTUS," WRITTEN BY ELIAS BOUDINOT AND PUBLISHED ON FEBRUARY 28, 1828

It has long been the opinion of judicious friends to the civilization of the Aborigines of America, that a paper published exclusively for the benefit, and under their direction, would add great force to the charitable means employed by the public for their melioration. In accordance with that opinion, the legislative authorities of the Cherokees have thought fit to patronize a weekly paper, bearing the above title [the *Cherokee Phoenix*]; and have appointed the subscriber to take charge of it as Editor. In issuing this Prospectus the Editor would, by no means, be too sanguine, for he is aware that he will tread upon *untried ground*: Nor does he make any pretentions to learning, for it must be known that the great and sole motive in establishing this paper, is the benifit of the Cherokees. This will be the great aim of the Editor, which he intends to pursue with undeviating steps. Many reasons might be given in support of the utility of such a paper as that which is now offered to the public, but it is deemed useless. There are many true friends to the Indians in different parts of the Union, who will rejoice to see this feeble effort of the Cherokees, to rise from their ashes, like the fabled Phoenix. On such friends must principally depend the support of our paper.

The Alphabet lately invented by a native Cherokee, of which the public have already been apprized, forms an interesting medium of information to those Cherokees who are unacquainted with the English language. For their benifit Cherokee types have been procured.

The columns of the Cherokee Phoenix will be filled, partly with English, and partly with Cherokee print; and all matter which is of common interest will be given in both languages in parallel columns.

As the great object of the Phoenix will be the benifit of the Cherokees, the following subjects will occupy its columns.

1. The laws and public documents of the Nation.

2. Account of the manners and customs of the Cherokees, and their progress in Education, Religion and the arts of civilized life; with such notices of other

Indian tribes as our limited means of information will allow.

3. The principal interesting news of the day.

4. Miscellaneous articles, calculated to promote Literature, Civilization, and Religion among the Cherokees.

In closing this short Prospectus, the Editor would appeal to the friends of Indians, and respectfully ask their patronage. Those who have heretofore manifested a christian zeal in promoting our welfare and happiness, will no doubt freely lend their helping hand.[14]

MURDER ANNOUNCEMENT, PUBLISHED MARCH 6, 1828

We are informed of a murder being committed in the neighborhood of Sumach. The name of the person killed is William Fallen, and of the murderer Bear's Paw. We have not heard of the circumstances.[15]

NOTICE, WRITTEN APRIL 30, 1828, PUBLISHED MAY 21, 1828

Taken up on Tarripin Creek, by Zachariah Simmons, on

the 19th inst. a BAY HORSE, with a small white on his fore-
head, about six years old, and five feet and two inches high,
and without any brand.

J. Vann

NOTICE, WRITTEN MAY 15, 1828,
PUBLISHED MAY 21, 1828

I hereby forewarn all persons against crediting my wife,
Delilah McConnell, on my account, as she has absconded without my consent. I am therefore determined to pay none of
her contracts.

William McConnell

NOTICES, PUBLISHED MAY 21, 1828

We are authorized to announce Richard Fields of Creek
Path, a Candidate for the Committee, for Chattooga District.

We are authorized to announce Messrs. Walter Adair and
John Ridge as Candidates for the Committee for Coosewattee
District. Also Major Ridge, Tesahdaski, and James Foster, as
Candidates for the Council for the same District.

We should like to receive the names of other Candidates.[16]

"Look Out for Rogues,"
published June 25, 1828

We understand that some person broke into the store of
Mr. Elijah Hicks last night, and helped himself to a number
of articles, such as pocket knives, shoes, boots, sugar, *whiskey*,
&c. It appears that the thief became so intoxicated before leaving the store as to forget his own shoes.[17]

Letter to the Editor,
published July 2, 1828

Ridge's Ferry, 24th April, 1828

Mr. Editor:——

We were again visited by death in the person of an eld-
erly Lady, OO-DAH-YEE, at the Savanna, 10 miles from here,
on the 22d inst. She was a woman distinguished through life
for honesty and industry, habits of application to Agricultural
pursuits, and the support of a large family, that would give to
any of the other sex a claim for admiration.—— Unassisted by
education, only in the knowledge of simple addition and sub-
traction which is within the reach of uncultivated minds, she,
by dint [of] application in farming and trading, had accumu-
lated a very handsome property, consisting of household furniture, mill, waggon, horses & cattle, sheep, Negro Slaves and
some money, all of which she has left to an only daughter and

three grand children, who are now called to mourn her loss. She died amidst friends in the wilderness, far from the consolations of religious guides, or those who could direct her to a Saviour. Her last words were, "I am gone before." I had a coffin made for her and sent to her from here, and before she was consigned to her long repose, I am informed, that all present took her by the hand and bid her adieu! She died of the Pleurisy.

John Ridge[18]

"INDIAN CLANS," ELIAS BOUDINOT EDITORIAL, PUBLISHED FEBRUARY 18, 1829

Most of our readers probably know what is meant by Indian clans. It is no more than a division of an Indian tribe into large families. We believe this custom is universal with the North American Indians. Among the Cherokees are seven clans, such as Wolf, Deer, Paint, &c. This simple division of the Cherokees formed the grand work by which marriages were regulated, and murder punished. A Cherokee could marry into any of the clans except two, that to which his father belongs, for all of that clan are his fathers and aunts, and that to which his mother belongs, for all of that clan are his brothers and sisters, a child invariably inheriting the clan of its mother. This custom which originated from time immemorial was observed with the greatest strictness. No law could be guarded and enforced with equal caution. In times past, the penalty annexed to it was not less than death. But it has scarcely, perhaps never been violated, except within a few years. Now it is invaded with impunity, though not to an equal extent with other customs of the Cherokees.

But it was the mutual law of clans as connected with murder, which rendered the custom savage and barbarous. We speak of what is was once, not as it is now, for the Cherokees, after experiencing sad effects from it, determined to, and did about twenty years ago in a solemn council, abolish it. From that time, murder has been considered a governmental crime.— Previous to that, the following were too palpably true, viz:

The Cherokees as a nation, had nothing to do with murder.

Murder was punished upon the principle of retaliation.

It belonged to the clan of the murdered to revenge his death.

If the murderer fled, his brother or nearest relative was liable to suffer in his stead.

If a man killed his brother, he was amenable to no law or clan.

If the murderer (this however is known only by tradition) was not as respectable as the murdered, his relative, or a man of his clan of a more respectable standing was liable to suffer.

To kill, under any circumstance whatever, was considered murder, and punished accordingly.

Our readers will say, "those were savage laws indeed." They were, and the Cherokees were then to be pitied, for the above were not mere inoperative laws, but were rigorously executed. But we can now say with pleasure, that they are all repealed, and are remembered only as vestiges of ignorance and barbarism.[19]

"CHEROKEE CHIEFS," LETTER TO THE EDITOR, PUBLISHED DECEMBER 3, 1831

Cherokee Nation
Nov. 24, 1831

Editor Of The *Cherokee Phoenix*,

For publication if you think proper, I send you a list of the names of the principal chiefs of the Cherokee Nation given by and from the memory of Noonday, an aged man. You will discover the dates of the times when each flourished are not given and which is impossible to obtain from any man "on the mortal side of existence." But in regard to some of these, a biographical sketch, highly interesting, may be written, by consulting our ancient men, who are still left to us as living monuments of other days; and historical books written by Americans and English. From various causes, of the last, we may not expect the whole truth or impartiality, but sufficient matter of fact can be gleaned, by tracing impressions made on their minds, from the eloquence and warlike deeds of our rude and savage, but in many respects, noble and lofty minded ancestors. To those who have the leisure may I recommend to write the life of Occunstota, whose chivalry is still cherished by our people, and who has been to this Nation, what Kosiusko [Polish patriot Thaddeus Kosciusko, who served as an American general in the Revolutionary War] has been to the also much oppressed Poland.

All of the chiefs mentioned in this list were seen by Noonday, except the first, who flourished before his recollection, but was well known to fame when he arrived at the age of discretion. His name was, *Etukkungsla*.

Occunstota succeeded this chief, and had for his vice chief, *Sahwanooka*, who administered the government as pricipal, when the first chief became very old, notwithstanding the old chief was exceedingly beloved, honored and well obeyed to the day of his death.

Under the administrations of the these two chiefs flourished the great war & civil chief called *Ataculculla* or *Woodleaning-up*, who is noticed in some of the British writers.

Eknngyeahdahhee, or the *Firstkiller* succeeded *Sahwonooka*, —to him succeeded the famous chief, ——

Kungnilla, or the *Little Turkey*, whose benignant influence at last achieved the establishment of durable treaties of peace with the United States. To this chief was addressed a friendly letter, written on vellum, and to which was attached a golden chain as an emblem of the purity of the faith of the United States, by [Henry] Dearborn, Secretary of war, acting under the special instruction of the President. After his death,

Enolee or the *Badger*, became the chief. In his time the people of the Nation became divided into parties, the civil and the vagrant, or as they are now well known by the designation of *"the lovers of the land,"* and "the Arkansas Emigration"

parties. Little was this chief qualified to tranquilize the discordant elements then rising into flame, or to oppose the malign influence of the United States officers, who blew the coal of contention, to enable themselves as friendly mediators to effect treaties in which the contending parties ceded large tracts of land by compromise and which enured to the advantage of the United States. The patriotic party, claiming themselves to be the representatives of forty and some odd towns deposed this chief, under the charge of bias to the Arkansas party & but in a subsequent Council of the nation he was reinstated to the dignity of the office, but from the wound inflicted upon his reputation he never recovered to the day of his death. Then commenced the administration of

Nungnoheeahdahkee or the *Pathkiller*, supported by *Charles R. Hicks*, who became the assistant principal chief, and other powerful chiefs, distinguished for their firmness, resolution, eloquence and wisdom, who effectually counteracted the tide of emigration opened by General [Andrew] Jackson, in the treaty of 1817, and closed the breach, by the last treaty of 1819, concluded with J. C. Calhoun then Secretary of war. The spirit of civilization infused itself in all the acts of the Nation, which now established a written code of laws in conformity with the advice and written instructions of President Jefferson to the Cherokee Nation. The Great Council was then divided into distinct bodies, with power to negative each others acts, and whose concurrence became necessary to the passage of any law. A Constitution was also recommended by these chiefs, which was made by a convention, the members of which were elected by the people. Previous to the operation of this

Constitution, and one year before the change was effected, it pleased the Great Spirit to call these good men, from the stage of human existence. To fill this vacancy, thus occasioned, for one year, devolved upon the members of the Council who held their seats, under the ancient and immemorial usage; who appointed by ballot, *William Hicks, Sen.* brother to the late *Charles R. Hicks*, to be the Principal chief, and *John Ross*, President of the Committee at that period to be the assistant principal chief. At the expiration of the term for which these chiefs were appointed, the members of the General Council, elected under the new Constitution, chose by ballot *John Ross* & *George Lowrey Sen.*; principal and assistant Principal chiefs, for four years, whose term of service will terminate in October, 1832.

Flying Cloud[20]

THE MANLY GAME
OF BALL-PLAYING, 1848

❧⟪❧⟪❧⟪❧⟪❧⟪❧⟪❧⟪❧⟪❧⟪❧⟪❧⟪❧⟪❧⟪❧⟪❧

Charles Lanman was born in Monroe, Michigan, in 1819. He spent several years in business before embarking on a literary career. Lanman wrote many books and contributed frequently to American and English journals. Washington Irving referred to him as "the picturesque explorer of the United States."[1]

In 1848, Lanman set out on a cross-country trek through the southern Appalachians that took him to Virginia, Georgia, Tennessee, and North Carolina. He wrote of the colorful characters and amazing geologic sights he saw along the way in a series of letters that was published in book form in 1849. During his journey, Lanman spent several weeks among the Cherokees recording legends and history as shared by their white leader, Colonel William Holland Thomas.

The 1848 visit to Qualla Town described in Lanman's *Letters from the Alleghany Mountains* came just ten years after the eastern Cherokee Nation was torn apart by the removal of most of the Cherokees to the West on the Trail of Tears. Thomas had successfully negotiated with the United States government for permission for the Qualla Cherokees to stay in North Carolina. He subsequently served as a main informant for visitors to Qualla Town, including Lanman in 1848 and James Mooney nearly forty years later.

From 1855 to 1857, Charles Lanman served as librarian of the Interior Department. In 1866, he became librarian of the House of Representatives. He also served as secretary to the Japanese Delegation in Washington from 1871 to 1882.[2]

What follows is one of Lanman's "letters" describing his visit with the Cherokees in 1848. In it, he describes watching a Cherokee ball game, which is similar to lacrosse, a game invented by Native Americans.

Excerpt from Charles Lanman's Letters from the Alleghany Mountains

Qualla Town, North Carolina, May, 1848

The plan adopted for the civilization of the Carolina Cherokees differs materially from any others adopted in the United States. Their amusements are not interfered with, excepting when found to have an immoral or unhappy tendency.

A goodly number of their more ridiculous games, however, they have abandoned of their own accord, but the manly game of *ball-playing* is still practised after the ancient manner, with one or two restrictions. In the first place, they are not allowed to wager their property on the games, as of old, unless it be some trifle in the way of a woollen belt or cotton handkerchief, and they are prohibited from choking each other, and breaking their heads and legs, when excited, as was their habit in former times. Since my arrival here the Indians have had one of their ball games, and as it was gotten up especially for my edification, I made it a point of etiquette to be present at the preparatory dance and the game, as well as at the concluding ceremony, and these I will now endeavor to describe.

The preparatory or training dance took place on the night preceding the game, and none participated in it who were not to play on the following day. There were sixty young men present, besides the spectators, and they met on a grassy plot formed by a bend of a neighboring stream called Soco Creek. The dancers were stripped of every particle of clothing but their waistbands; they made their own music, which was composed merely of a rapid succession of whoops and shouts; and they danced round a large blazing fire. The night in question was very beautiful, and when this strange group was looked upon by the light of the full moon, and the wild mountain scenery on every side, they presented a most romantic appearance indeed. They kept up the dance for over an hour, and, when it was concluded, all the men immediately ran towards a deep pool in the ice-cold stream, and without waiting for the perspiration to cool, plunged into the water, and, having finally emerged, started for their several homes. This dance, I am informed, had its origin in an ancient custom, which compelled all the candidates for a game of ball to inure themselves to every hardship for ten days before the game took place, and during all that time they were to eat but little food, and were to refrain from gratifying any of their sensual appetites.

On the morning of the game a large plain, lying between two hills and directly in front of the Indian Courthouse, (a large circular lodge, built of logs,) was divested of every stone and stick on its surface, and at ten o'clock the spectators began to assemble. These were composed of the old men of the nation, a large number of boys, and a still larger number of women and children. They were all dressed in their holiday attire, so that feathers, shawl turbans, scarlet belts, and gaudy hunting shirts were quite abundant; and, scattered as they were in groups of from five to fifty on the hill sides and under the shadow of the trees, they presented a most picturesque appearance. During all this time the players had kept out of sight, and it was understood that the two parties were among the bushes, at the two ends of the plain, preparing themselves for the game. Under the direction of the presiding chief or game-director, two poles were now erected about six hundred yards apart, on either side of a given centre, and in this centre was placed the ball. From this point was the ball to be given to the players, and the party which first succeeded in throwing it outside of the pole belonging to their opponents to the number of twelve times were to be considered the winners.

Every thing being ready, a shrill whoop was given from one end of the plain, and immediately answered by the opposing party, when they all made their appearance, marching slowly to the centre, shouting and yelling as they passed along. Each party consisted of thirty splendidly formed young men, who were unincumbered by any clothing, save their common waistband, and every individual carried in his hand a pair of ball sticks, made with a braided bag at one end. As the parties approached the centre, the ladyloves of the players ran out upon the plain and gave their favorite champions a variety of articles, such as belts and handkerchiefs, which they were willing to wager upon the valor of their future husbands. This little movement struck me as particularly interesting, and I was greatly pleased with the bashfulness and yet complete confidence with which the Indian maidens manifested their preferences.

When the several parties were assembled at the centre of the plain, each man selected his particular antagonist by placing his sticks at his rival's feet, after which the game-director delivered a long speech, wherein he warned them to adhere to the existing regulations; and, throwing the ball high up in the air, made his escape to one side of the plain, and the game commenced. As it proceeded, the players became greatly excited, and I noticed that the ball was never taken in hand until after it had been picked up by the *spoony* stick, but the expertness with which these movements were performed was indeed surprising. At one time the whole crowd of players would rush together in the most desperate and fearful manner, presenting, as they struggled for the ball, the appearance of a dozen gladiators, striving to overcome a monster serpent; and then again, as one man would secure the ball and start for the boundary line of his opponent, the races which ensued were very beautiful and exciting. Wrestling conflicts also occurred quite frequently, and it often seemed as if the players would break every bone in their bodies as they threw each other in the air, or dragged each other over the ground; and many of the leaps, which single individuals performed, were really superb. The exercise was of a character that would kill the majority of white men. The game lasted for about two hours, and the moment it was finished the entire body of players, while yet panting with excessive fatigue, made a rush for the neighboring river, and in a short time appeared on the plain in their usual garb, and the old chief who had held the stakes awarded the prizes to the winning party. A short time afterwards the boys stripped themselves, and went through the same routine of playing as already described, when the ball-playing was at an end, and the people began to disperse with a view of getting ready for the evening dance.

I employed the intervening time by going home with one of the chiefs, and eating a comfortable supper in his log cabin. The habitation of this chief was made of hewn logs, and occupied a farm of twenty acres on the mountain side, about one-fourth of which was in a state of cultivation, and planted with corn and potatoes. He had a tidy wife and several children, and his stock consisted of a pony, a cow, and some ten or a dozen sheep. At nine o'clock, I was again in the midst of a crowd of Indians, assembled at the court-house of the town.

The edifice, so called, is built of hewn logs, very large and circular, without any floor but that of solid earth, and without any seats but one short bench intended for the great men of the nation. In the centre of this lodge was a large fire, and the number of persons who figured in the several dances of the evening, was perhaps two hundred, all fantastically dressed, and including men, women, and boys. Each dancer made his own music, and, with one exception, the dances were of the common Indian sort. The exception alluded to was particularly fantastic, and called "the Pilgrim Dance." They came in with packs on their backs, with their faces strangely painted, and with gourds hanging at their sides, and the idea seemed to be to represent their hospitality towards all strangers who visited them from distant lands. The dancing continued until midnight, when the presiding chief addressed the multitude on the subject of their duties as intelligent beings, and told them to return to their several homes and resume their labors in the field and in the shops. He concluded by remarking that he hoped I was pleased with what I had witnessed, and trusted that nothing had happened which would make the wise men of my country in the East think less of the poor Indian than they did at the present time: and he then added that, according to an ancient custom, as I was a stranger they liked, the several chiefs had given me a name, by which I should hereafter be remembered among the Carolina Cherokees, and that name was *Ga-taw-hough No-que-sih*, or *The Wandering Star*.[3]

SOUND FROM THE DISTANT MOUNTAINS
THE CHEROKEE STORYTELLERS, 1887–90

❧❦❧❦❧❦❧❦❧❦❧❦❧❦❧❦❧❦❧❦❧❦❧❦❧❦

When James Mooney of the Bureau of American Ethnology went to live with the Cherokees in 1887, he was only twenty-six. Mooney lived with the Cherokees for parts of the years from 1887 to 1890 and for interim periods later. The eager young man immersed himself in the language and traditions of the Cherokees and engaged their elders and shamans to help him document their history, culture, and sacred practices for posterity.[1]

Mooney's chief informant was A'yûn'inĭ, or Swimmer, who was born about 1835 and was raised to become a shaman and a keeper of Cherokee traditions. He served in the Confederate army as a second sergeant under Colonel William Holland Thomas, the white leader of the North Carolina Cherokees. Mooney described Swimmer as a "genuine aboriginal antiquarian and patriot, proud of his people and their ancient system, he took delight in recording in his native alphabet the songs and sacred formulas of priests and dancers and the names of medicinal plants and the prescriptions with which they were compounded, while his mind was a storehouse of Indian tradition."[2]

Mooney coaxed Swimmer into sharing his manuscript of sacred Cherokee formulas with him. Swimmer made a copy of the formulas, written in the Cherokee alphabet, and gave it to Mooney to place in the Smithsonian for preservation.[3] Swimmer died in March 1899 and was buried "on the slope of a forest-clad mountain," according to Mooney. "With him perished half the tradition of a people," Mooney said of his friend's death.[4]

Ităgû′năhĭ, or John Ax, was born about 1800 and was still living when Mooney's *Myths of the Cherokee* was published in 1900. By the age of nineteen, John Ax was married and a father. While he was not trained to be a shaman, as Swimmer was, John Ax was recognized by the Cherokees as an authority on tribal customs. Mooney described him as being of a poetic and imaginative temperament and as being skilled at making rattles, wands, and ceremonial instruments. He collected stories of enormous snakes, invisible beings, and ugly giants.[5]

James Mooney has been given much credit for recording and preserving the wonderful stories, beliefs, and formulas of the Cherokees. And while his contribution is very significant, more credit should be given Swimmer, John Ax, Gahuni, and other Cherokees for preserving the traditions through years of turmoil and assimilation into the world of the white man. Many stories and sacred formulas for curing ills, improving the hunt, luck in ball-play and love, and other aspects of daily life were written in the Cherokee syllabary invented by Sequoyah and jealously guarded by the writers and their families. Other traditions were consigned to memory and passed on through a strong oral tradition.[6] Mooney's contribution in translating them into English and publishing them was invaluable, but the original conservators of the rich traditions were the Cherokee elders and shamans.

Below is a selection of Cherokee legends recorded by Mooney.

The version of the "First Fire" legend presented here was told to Mooney by Swimmer and John Ax. Mooney heard alternate versions of the story from other sources. In one version, the Dragon-fly assists the Water Spider by pushing the *tusti* bowl from behind. In a corresponding Creek myth, the rabbit is responsible for stealing the fire.[7]

The second story, "The Ice Man," was obtained from Swimmer. Mooney speculated it was based on a tradition of a coal mine that was accidentally set on fire as the result of the Cherokee practice of burning the woods in the fall to enhance the wildlife habitat for hunting.[8]

The first story in "The Removed Townhouses" was obtained from John Ax, while the second was told by Salâ′lĭ, or Squirrel.[9] Squirrel was not a primary contributor to Mooney's collection but was an interesting person nonetheless. Charles Lanman described Squirrel in 1848 as "quite a young man" with "a remarkably thoughtful face. He is the blacksmith of this nation, and with some assistance supplies the whole of Qualla Town with all their axes and plows; but what is more, he has manufactured a number of very superior rifles and pistols, including stock, barrel, and lock, and he is also the builder of grist mills, which grind all the corn which his people eat. A specimen of his workmanship in the way of a rifle may be seen at the Patent Office in Washington, where it was deposited by Mr. [William Holland] Thomas; and I believe Salola [Squirrel] is the first Indian who ever manufactured an entire gun. But when it is remembered that he never received a particle of education in any of the mechanic arts but is entirely self-taught, his attainments must be considered truly remarkable." Squirrel, who was married to a Catawba woman, died about 1895.[10]

The Nûñně′hǐ, also known as the Immortals, are the heroes in "The Removed Townhouses." They are described by Mooney not as ghosts, but as a race of invisible spirit people, as sometimes mischievous, sometimes benevolent supernatural human beings. They figure in several Cherokee myths, often appearing to rescue or aid the Cherokees in times of trouble. Mooney said that one of his informants, James D. Wafford, clearly believed in the existence of the Immortals.[11] All of the locations described in "The Removed Townhouses" are in North Carolina, except for Gustǐ′ in East Tennessee.[12]

"The First Fire"

In the beginning there was no fire, and the world was cold, until the Thunders (Ani´-Hyûñ´tĭkwălâ´skĭ), who lived up in Gălûñ´lătĭ, sent their lightning and put fire into the bottom of a hollow sycamore tree which grew on an island. The animals knew it was there, because they could see the smoke coming out at the top, but they could not get to it on account of the water, so they held a council to decide what to do. This was a long time ago.

Every animal that could fly or swim was anxious to go after the fire. The Raven offered, and because he was so large and strong they thought he could surely do the work, so he was sent first. He flew high and far across the water and alighted on the sycamore tree, but while he was wondering what to do next, the heat had scorched all his feathers black, and he was frightened and came back without the fire. The little Screech-owl (Wa´huhu´) volunteered to go, and reached the place safely, but while he was looking down into the hollow tree a blast of hot air came up and nearly burned out his eyes. He managed to fly home as best he could, but it was a long time before he could see well, and his eyes are red to this day. Then the Hooting Owl (U´guku´) and the Horned Owl (Tskĭlĭ´) went, but by the time they got to the hollow tree the fire was burning so fiercely that the smoke nearly blinded them, and the ashes carried up by the wind made white rings about their eyes. They had to come home again without the fire, but with all their rubbing they were never able to get rid of the white rings.

Now no more of the birds would venture, and so the little Uksu´hĭ snake, the black racer, said he would go through the water and bring back some fire. He swam across to the island and crawled through the grass to the tree, and went in by a small hole at the bottom. The heat and smoke were too much for him, too, and after dodging about blindly over the hot ashes until he was almost on fire himself he managed by good luck to get out again at the same hole, but his body had been scorched black, and he has ever since had the habit of darting and doubling on his track as if trying to escape from close quarters. He came back, and the great blacksnake, Gûle´gĭ, "The Climber," offered to go for fire. He swam over to the island and climbed up the tree on the outside, as the blacksnake always does, but when he put his head down into the hole the smoke choked him so that he fell into the burning stump, and before he could climb out again he was as black as the Uksu´hĭ.

Now they held another council, for still there was no fire, and the world was cold, but birds, snakes, and four-footed animals, all had some excuse for not going, because they were all afraid to venture near the burning sycamore, until at last Kănăne´skĭ Amaĭ´yĕhĭ (the Water Spider) said she would go. This is not the water spider that looks like a mosquito, but the other one, with black downy hair and red stripes on her body. She can run on top of the water or dive to the bottom, so there would be no trouble to get over to the island, but the question was, How could she bring back the fire? "I'll manage that," said the Water Spider; so she spun a thread from her body and wove it into a *tusti* bowl, which she fastened on her back. Then she crossed over to the island and through the grass to where the fire was still burning. She put one little coal of fire into her bowl, and came back with it, and ever since we have had fire, and the Water Spider still keeps her tusti bowl.[13]

"The Ice Man"

Once when the people were burning the woods in the fall the blaze set fire to a poplar tree, which continued to burn until the fire went down into the roots and burned a great hole in the ground. It burned and burned, and the hole grew constantly larger, until the people became frightened and were afraid it would burn the whole world. They tried to put out the fire, but it had gone too deep, and they did not know what to do.

At last some one said there was a man living in a house of ice far in the north who could put out the fire, so messengers were sent, and after traveling a long distance they came to the ice house and found the Ice Man at home. He was a little fellow with long hair hanging down to the ground in two plaits. The messengers told him their errand and he at once said, "O yes, I can help you," and began to unplait his hair. When it was all unbraided he took it up in one hand and struck it once across his other hand, and the messengers felt a wind blow against their cheeks. A second time he struck his hair across his hand, and a light rain began to fall. The third time he struck his hair across his open hand there was sleet mixed with the raindrops, and when he struck the fourth time great hailstones fell upon the ground, as if they had come out from the ends of his hair. "Go back now," said the Ice Man, "and I shall be there to-morrow." So the messengers returned to their people, whom they found still gathered helplessly about the great burning pit.

The next day while they were all watching about the fire there came a wind from the north, and they were afraid, for they knew that it came from the Ice Man. But the wind only made the fire blaze up higher. Then a light rain began to fall, but the drops seemed only to make the fire hotter. Then the shower turned to a heavy rain, with sleet and hail that killed the blaze and made clouds of smoke and steam rise from the red coals. The people fled to their homes for shelter, and the storm rose to a whirlwind that drove the rain into every burning crevice and piled great hailstones over the embers, until the fire was dead and even the smoke ceased. When at last it was all over and the people returned they found a lake where the burning pit had been, and from below the water came a sound as of embers still crackling.[14]

"The Removed Townhouses"

Long ago, long before the Cherokee were driven from their homes in 1838, the people on Valley river and Hiwassee heard voices of invisible spirits in the air calling and warning them of wars and misfortunes which the future held in store, and inviting them to come and live with the Nûñnĕ′hĭ, the

Immortals, in their homes under the mountains and under the waters. For days the voices hung in the air, and the people listened until they heard the spirits say, "If you would live with us, gather everyone in your townhouses and fast there for seven days, and no one must raise a shout or a warwhoop in all that time. Do this and we shall come and you will see us and we shall take you to live with us."

The people were afraid of the evils that were to come, and they knew that the Immortals of the mountains and the waters were happy forever, so they counciled in their townhouses and decided to go with them. Those of Anisgayâ′yǐ town came all together into their townhouse and prayed and fasted for six days. On the seventh day there was a sound from the distant mountains, and it came nearer and grew louder until a roar of thunder was all about the townhouse and they felt the ground shake under them. Now they were frightened, and despite the warning some of them screamed out. The Nûñně′hǐ, who had already lifted up the townhouse with its mound to carry it away, were startled by the cry and let a part of it fall to the earth, where now we see the mound of Sě′tsǐ. They steadied themselves again and bore the rest of the townhouse, with all the people in it, to the top of Tsuda′ye′lûñ′yǐ (Lone peak), near the head of Cheowa, where we can still see it, changed long ago to solid rock, but the people are invisible and immortal.

The people of another town, on Hiwassee, at the place which we call now Du′stiya′lûñ′yǐ, where Shooting creek comes in, also prayed and fasted, and at the end of seven days the Nûñně′hǐ came and took them away down under the water. They are there now, and on a warm summer day, when the wind ripples the surface, those who listen well can hear them talking below. When the Cherokee drag the river for fish the fish-drag always stops and catches there, although the water is deep, and the people know it is being held by their lost kinsmen, who do not want to be forgotten.

When the Cherokee were forcibly removed to the West one of the greatest regrets of those along Hiwassee and Valley rivers was that they were compelled to leave behind forever their relatives who had gone to the Nûñnĕ′hĭ.

In Tennessee river, near Kingston, 18 miles below Loudon, Tennessee, is a place which the Cherokee call Gustĭ′, where there once was a settlement long ago, but one night while the people were gathered in the townhouse for a dance the bank caved in and carried them all down into the river. Boatmen passing the spot in their canoes see the round dome of the townhouse—now turned to stone—in the water below them and sometimes hear the sound of the drum and dance coming up, and they never fail to throw food into the water in return for being allowed to cross in safety.[15]

NOTES

❧❦❧❦❧❦❧❦❧❦❧❦❧❦❧❦❧❦❧❦❧❦❧❦❧❦❧❦

Hands and Hearts Joined Together

1. Stanley W. Hoig, *The Cherokees and Their Chiefs* (Fayetteville: The University of Arkansas Press, 1998), 17-18.
2. Alexander Cuming, *Memoirs of the Life of Alexander Cuming*, Cherokee Documents in Foreign Archives, Special Collections, Hunter Library, Add 39855, sch. no. 65528, Microfilm #172, 25; Hoig, *The Cherokees and Their Chiefs*, 19.
3. Matthew Allen Newsome, "Alexander Cuming: An Examination of Contemporary Documents," (1998), http: // www.scottishtartans.org / cuming.html; Cuming, *Memoirs*, 25-28; Hoig, *The Cherokees and Their Chiefs*, 19.

4. Newsome, "Alexander Cuming;" William O. Steele, *The Cherokee Crown of Tannassy* (Winston-Salem, N.C.: John F. Blair, Publisher 1977), 23-24, 31-33; Cuming, *Memoirs*, 25; Hoig, *The Cherokees and Their Chiefs*, 9-10, 19-20.

5. Newsome, "Alexander Cuming;" Cuming, *Memoirs*, 25.

6. Hoig, *The Cherokees and Their Chiefs,* 20.

7. Steele, *The Cherokee Crown of Tannassy*, 66-70; Newsome, "Alexander Cuming;" Cuming, *Memoirs*, 25; Hoig, *The Cherokees and Their Chiefs*, 19.

8. Hoig, *The Cherokees and Their Chiefs,* 20; Cuming, *Memoirs*, 26-27; Newsome, "Alexander Cuming;" Steele, *The Cherokee Crown of Tannassy*, 109-13.

9. Alexander Cuming, *Memorials of Alexander Cuming to King George*, Cherokee Documents in Foreign Archives, Special Collections, Hunter Library, CO54, 06442, Microfilm #197, 219, 222; Newsome, "Alexander Cuming;" Cuming, *Memoirs*, 27-28.

10. Newsome, "Alexander Cuming;" Cuming, *Memoirs*, 4.

11. Hoig, *The Cherokees and Their Chiefs,* 22-23.

12. "Articles of Friendship & Commerce," Cherokee Documents in Foreign Archives, Special Collections, Hunter Library, CO54, 06442, Microfilm #197, 211-14.

13. "Answer of the Indian Chiefs," Cherokee Documents in Foreign Archives, Special Collections, Hunter Library, CO54, 06442, Microfilm # 197, 215-16.

14. Cuming, *Memoirs,* 25-28.

The Price of a White Shirt

1. *Colonial Records of South Carolina: Journals of the Commissioners of the Indian Trade*, Microfilm, 321.
2. David H. Corkran, *The Cherokee Frontier: Conflict and Survival, 1740-62* (Norman: The University of Oklahoma Press, 1962), 40-42.
3. Corkran, *The Cherokee Frontier*, 43-44.
4. *Colonial Records,* 173.
5. Ibid., 299-308.

A Second Peace

1. E. Raymond Evans, "Notable Persons in Cherokee History: Ostenaco," *Journal of Cherokee Studies.* Vol. 1 No. 1, Summer, 1976, 46-47; Corkran, *Cherokee Frontier*, 219-21.
2. Henry Timberlake, *The Memoirs of Lieut. Henry Timberlake* (London, printed for the author, 1765), 10-11; Corkran, *Cherokee Frontier*, 265-66.
3. Evans, "Notable Persons," 47, 53; Timberlake, *Memoirs*, 13, 16.
4. Evans, "Notable Persons," 47-48; Timberlake, *Memoirs*, 112.
5. Evans, "Notable Persons," 51; Timberlake, *Memoirs*, 125.
6. Evans, "Notable Persons," 51.
7. Ibid., 53.
8. Timberlake, *Memoirs*, 29-35.
9. Ibid., 83-96.

Welcome in their Country as a Friend and Brother

1. William Bartram, *Travels through North and South Carolina, Georgia, East &West Florida . . .*, 1791 (Reprint, London: for James Johnson, 1792), 329.
2. Hoig, *The Cherokees and Their Chiefs*, 42.
3. Bartram, *Travels*, 362-70.
4. Ibid., 371-72.

Too Near the Shore

1. Samuel Cole Williams, *Early Travels in the Tennessee Country: 1540-1800,* 1928 (Reprint, Nashville: Franklin Book Reprints, 1970), 231-32; Grace Steele Woodward, *The Cherokees*, 1963 (Norman and London, University of Oklahoma Press, 10th printing, 1988), 88-89, 97; Hoig, *The Cherokees and Their Chiefs*, 58-59; Samuel Cole Williams, *Dawn of the Tennessee Valley and Tennessee History* (Johnson City, Tenn.: Watauga Press, 1937), 402-4.
2. Woodward, *The Cherokees*, 100; Hoig, *The Cherokees and Their Chiefs*, 64-65; Emmet Starr, *History of the Cherokee Indians and Their Legends and Folk Lore*, 1921 (Reprint, Millwood, N.Y.: Kraus Reprint Co., 1977), 33.
3. Williams, *Early Travels*, 231-32; J. G. M. Ramsey, *The Annals of Tennessee to the End of the Eighteenth Century* (Philadelphia: J. B. Lippincott & Co., 1860), 196-206.

4. Williams, *Early Travels*, 231-32; Carolyn Sakowski, *Touring the East Tennessee Backroads*, 1993 (2nd Printing, Winston-Salem, N.C.: John F. Blair, Publisher, 1997), 160-62.

5. *Goodspeed's General History of Tennessee*, 1887 (Reprint, Nashville: Charles and Randy Elder, Booksellers, 1973), 134-35; Ramsey, *The Annals of Tennessee,* 200.

6. Ramsey, *The Annals of Tennessee,* 198-202.

A Pipe and a Little Tobacco

1. Hoig, *The Cherokees and Their Chiefs*, 277 n15, 278 n14.

2. Ibid., 62.

3. Hoig, *The Cherokees and Their Chiefs*, 68; James Mooney, *James Mooney's History, Myths, and Sacred Formulas of the Cherokees* (Asheville, N.C.: Historical Images, 1992), Introduction by George Ellison, 61-62; Charles C. Royce, "The Cherokee Nation of Indians," *Fifth Annual Report of the Bureau of Ethnology to the Secretary of the Smithsonian Institution* (Washington: Government Printing Office, 1887), 133-34.

4. Hoig, *The Cherokees and Their Chiefs*, 70; Mooney, *James Mooney's History*, 63-64; Royce, "The Cherokee Nation," 152.

5. Hoig, *The Cherokees and Their Chiefs*, 72.

6. Ibid., 14-15.

7. *American State Papers: Class II, Indian Affairs*, (Washington, D. C.: Gales and Seaton, 1832), 1:41.

8. Ibid., 1:40-42.

Blood is Spilt at Both of our Houses

1. Hoig, *The Cherokees and Their Chiefs*, 65.
2. Ibid., 74-75.
3. Hoig, *The Cherokees and Their Chiefs*, 80, 85; *American State Papers*, 1:459.
4. *American State Papers*, 1:363.
5. Hoig, *The Cherokees and Their Chiefs*, 88, 90.
6. *American State Papers*, 1:459-61.
7. Ibid., 1:464.

According to the Law of This Country

1. Henry Thompson Malone, "Return Jonathan Meigs: Indian Agent Extraordinary." *East Tennessee Historical Society's Publications*, 28 (1956): 4-5.
2. Malone, "Return J. Meigs," 5, 7.
3. Ibid., 5, 14, 22.
4. Lela Latch Lloyd, *If the Chief Vann House Could Speak* (Abilene, Tex.: printed by Quality Printing Co., 1980), 4, 7-9; Hoig, *The Cherokees and Their Chiefs*, 94.
5. Malone, "Return J. Meigs," 8; Lloyd, *If the Chief Vann House, 6;* Hoig, *The Cherokees and Their Chiefs*, 91.
6. Lloyd, *If the Chief Vann House, 8;* Hoig, *The Cherokees and Their*

Chiefs, 93-94.

7. Malone, "Return J. Meigs," 8.

8. Lloyd, *If the Chief Vann House, 9;* Hoig, *The Cherokees and Their Chiefs*, 98.

9. Return J. Meigs, *Daybook #2*, Photocopy of original, Chatta-nooga-Hamilton County Bicentennial Library, Acc. No. 283, Box11, eleven folders labeled "Cherokee Indian Agency, 1801-1807," 65.

10. Ibid., 73-74.

11. Ibid., 215-16.

12. Ibid., 217-18.

13. Ibid., 219-20.

14. Ibid., 221-22.

15. Ibid., 223-24.

16. Ibid., 225-27.

17. Ibid., 228.

An Ardent Zeal

1. Robert Sparks Walker, *Torchlights to the Cherokees: The Brainerd Mission* (New York: The MacMillan Company, 1931), 28-29, 31, 42, 60, 105, 107, 329-31; Daniel S. Butrick, *The Journal of Rev. Daniel S. Butrick: May 19, 1838–April 1, 1839* (Park Hill, Okla.: Trail of Tears Association, 1998), 33, 36.

2. Rev. Rufus Anderson, *Memoir of Catharine Brown, A Christian Indian, of the Cherokee Nation* (University, Ala.: Confederate

Publishing Company, 1986), Intro. & ed. William Stanley
Hoole, 3-6, 9, 14-15, 22, 26-27; Walker, *Torchlights*, 154-55,
175-76, 179-85.

3. Walker, *Torchlights*, 44.

4. Isaac Anderson, Matthew Donald, and David Campbell,
Letter to the American Board of Commissioners for Foreign
Missions dated May 29, 1818, original letter in a folder titled
"American Board of Commissioners for Foreign Missions" on
file at the Chattanooga-Hamilton County Bicentennial
Library, ACC. No. 153, Box 8, 4 pages.

5. Catharine Brown, Letter from Catharine Brown to the
Chamberlains, original letter in folder titled "Brown,
Catherine. Fort Deposit, Alabama. December 12, 1818; To
Mr. and Mrs. William Chamberlain, Brainerd," on file at the
Chattanooga-Hamilton County Bicentennial Library, Acc.
No. 117, Box 7.

To Rise from Their Ashes

1. Elias Boudinot, *Cherokee Editor: The Writings of Elias Boudinot*,
Ed. Theda Perdue (Knoxville: University of Tennessee Press,
1983), 11, 13; *Cherokee Phoenix*, 21 Feb. 1828: 4; Grant
Foreman, *Sequoyah*, 1938 (2d printing, Norman: University
of Oklahoma Press, 1959), 11, 39.

2. Boudinot, *Cherokee Editor*, 15.

3. Starr, *History of the Cherokee Indians*, 113.

4. Elias Boudinot, "Prospectus," *Cherokee Phoenix*, 28 Feb. 1828: 2.

5. Boudinot, *Cherokee Editor*, 87.

6. Ibid., 15-16.

7. Boudinot, *Cherokee Editor*, 145; Boudinot, *Cherokee Phoenix*, 6 May 1828.

8. Thurman Wilkins, *Cherokee Tragedy: The Story of the Ridge Family and the Decimation of a People*, 1970 (2nd ed., Norman and London: University of Oklahoma Press, 1970), 244-45; Boudinot, *Cherokee Editor*, 25-26.

9. Gary E. Moulton, *John Ross: Cherokee Chief* (Athens: University of Georgia Press, 1978), 65; Wilkins, *Cherokee Tragedy*, 280-21.

10. Starr, *History*, 95.

11. Starr, *History*, 95; Wilkins, *Cherokee Tragedy*, 335-39.

12. Wilkins, *Cherokee Tragedy*, 333-35, 339.

13. Wilkins, *Cherokee Tragedy*, 99-107, 189, 216; Walker, *Torchlights*, 156.

14. Boudinot, "Prospectus," *Cherokee Phoenix*, 28 Feb. 1828: 2.

15. *Cherokee Phoenix*, 6 Mar. 1828: 3.

16. Ibid., 21 May 1828: 3.

17. Ibid., 25 June 1828: 2.

18. Ibid., 2 July 1828: 3.

19. Elias Boudinot, "Indian Clans," *Cherokee Phoenix and Indian's Advocate*, 18 Feb. 1829: 2.

20. Flying Cloud, letter to the Editor, *Cherokee Phoenix and Indian's Advocate*, 3 Dec. 1831: 2.

The Manly Game of Ball-playing

1. James Grant Wilson and John Fiske, eds., *Appleton's Cyclopaedia of American Biography*, Vol. III (N.Y.: D. Appleton & Co., 1887), 614.
2. Ibid.
3. Charles Lanman, *Letters from the Alleghany Mountains* (New York: George P. Putnam, 1849), 100-105.

Sound from the Distant Mountains

1. Mooney, *James Mooney's History*, 2; James Mooney, "Myths of the Cherokee," *Nineteenth Annual Report of the Bureau of American Ethnology* (Washington, D.C.: Government Printing Office, 1900), 11.
2. Mooney, "Myths of the Cherokee," 236.
3. James Mooney, "The Sacred Formulas of the Cherokees," *Seventh Annual Report of the Bureau of Ethnology* (Washington, D.C.: Government Printing Office, 1891), 310-12.
4. Mooney, "Myths of the Cherokee," 236-37.
5. Ibid., 237.
6. Mooney, "Sacred Formulas of the Cherokees," 307-14.
7. Mooney, "Myths of the Cherokee," 431.
8. Ibid., 470.
9. Ibid., 476.
10. Lanman, *Letters from the Alleghany Mountains,* 111; Mooney,

"Myths of the Cherokee," 166-67, 237.

11. Mooney, "Myths of the Cherokee," 475.

12. Ibid., 476.

13. Ibid., 240-42.

14. Ibid., 322-23.

15. Ibid., 335-36.

BIBLIOGRAPHY

American State Papers: Class II, Indian Affairs. Vol. 1. Washington D.C.: Gales and Seaton, 1832.

Anderson, Rufus. *Memoir of Catharine Brown, A Christian Indian, of the Cherokee Nation.* Edited and with an introduction by William Stanley Hoole. University, Ala.: Confederate Publishing Co., 1986.

"Answer of the Indian Chiefs." Cherokee Documents in Foreign Archives, Special Collections, Hunter Library. C054, 06442, Microfilm #197.

"Articles of Friendship & Commerce." Cherokee Documents in Foreign Archives, Special Collections, Hunter Library. C054, 06442, Microfilm #197.

Bartram, William. *Travels through North and South Carolina, Georgia, East &West Florida. . . .* 1791. Reprint, London: for James Johnson, 1792.

Boudinot, Elias. *Cherokee Editor: The Writings of Elias Boudinot*. Edited by Theda Perdue. Knoxville: University of Tennessee Press, 1983.

Butrick, Daniel S. *The Journal of Rev. Daniel S. Butrick: May 19, 1838-April 1, 1839*. Park Hill, Okla.: Trail of Tears Association, 1998.

Chattanooga-Hamilton County Bicentennial Library, Chattanooga, Tenn. Special Collections. Folders entitled "American Board of Commissioners for Foreign Missions," "Brown, Catherine," and "Cherokee Indian Agency, 1801-1807."

Cherokee Phoenix, 28 February 1828—3 December 1831.

Colonial Records of South Carolina: Journals of the Commissioners of the Indian Trade. Microfilm, 321.

Corkran, David H. *The Cherokee Frontier: Conflict and Survival, 1740-62*. Norman: University of Oklahoma Press, 1962.

Cuming, Alexander. *Memoirs of the Life of Alexander Cuming*. Cherokee Documents in Foreign Archives, Special Collections, Hunter Library. Add 39855, sch. no. 65528, Microfilm #172.

———. *Memorials of Alexander Cuming to King George*. Cherokee Documents in Foreign Archives, Special Collections, Hunter Library. CO54, 06442, Microfilm #197.

Evans, E. Raymond. "Notable Persons in Cherokee History: Ostenaco." *Journal of Cherokee Studies* Vol. 1, No. 1 (Summer 1976).

Foreman, Grant. *Sequoyah*. 1938. Second printing, Norman: University of Oklahoma Press, 1959.

Goodspeed's General History of Tennessee. 1887. Reprint, Nashville: Charles and Randy Elder, Booksellers, 1973.

Hoig, Stanley W. *The Cherokees and Their Chiefs*. Fayetteville: The University of Arkansas Press, 1998.

Hunter Library, Western Carolina University, Cullowhee, N.C. Special Collections. Cherokee Documents in Foreign Archives.

Lanman, Charles. *Letters from the Alleghany Mountains*. New York: George P. Putnam, 1849.

Lloyd, Lela Latch. *If the Chief Vann House Could Speak*. Abilene, Tex.: Quality Printing Co., 1980.

Malone, Henry Thompson. "Return Jonathan Meigs: Indian Agent Extraordinary." *East Tennessee Historical Society's Publications,* 28 (1956): 3-22.

Mooney, James. *James Mooney's History, Myths, and Sacred Formulas of the Cherokees*. Asheville, N.C.: Historical Images, 1992.

———. "Myths of the Cherokee." *19th Annual Report of the Bureau of American Ethnology*. Washington, D.C.: Government Printing Office, 1900.

———. "Sacred Formulas of the Cherokees." *7th Annual Report of the Bureau of Ethnology*. Washington, D.C.: Government Printing Office, 1891.

Moulton, Gary E. *John Ross: Cherokee Chief*. Athens: University of Georgia Press, 1978.

Newsome, Matthew Allen. "Alexander Cuming: An Examination of Contemporary Documents." 1998. http://www.scottishtartans.org/cuming.html.

Ramsey, J. G. M. *The Annals of Tennessee to the End of the Eighteenth Century*. Philadelphia: J. B. Lippincott and Co., 1860.

Royce, Charles C. "The Cherokee Nation of Indians: A Narrative of Their Official Relations with the Colonial and Federal

Governments." *5th Annual Report of the Bureau of Ethnology to the Secretary of the Smithsonian Institution*. Washington, D.C.: Government Printing Office, 1887.

Sakowski, Carolyn. *Touring the East Tennessee Backroads*. 1993. Second printing, Winston-Salem, N.C.: John F. Blair, Publisher, 1997.

Starr, Emmet. *History of the Cherokee Indians and Their Legends and Folk Lore*. 1921. Reprint, Millwood, N.Y.: Kraus Reprint Co., 1977.

Steele, William O. *The Cherokee Crown of Tannassy*. Winston-Salem, N.C.: John F. Blair, Publisher, 1977.

Timberlake, Henry. *The Memoirs of Lieut. Henry Timberlake*. London: privately printed, 1765.

Walker, Robert Sparks. *Torchlights to the Cherokees: The Brainerd Mission*. New York: The Macmillan Company, 1931.

Wilkins, Thurman. *Cherokee Tragedy: The Story of the Ridge Family and the Decimation of a People*. 2d ed. Norman and London: University of Oklahoma Press, 1970.

Williams Samuel Cole. *Dawn of the Tennessee Valley and Tennessee History*. Johnson City, Tenn.: Watauga Press, 1937.

————. *Early Travels in the Tennessee Country: 1540-1800*. 1928. Reprint, Nashville: Franklin Book Reprints, 1970.

Wilson, James Grant, and John Fiske, eds. *Appleton's Cyclopaedia of American Biography*. Vol. 3. New York: D. Appleton and Co., 1887.

Woodward, Grace Steele. *The Cherokees*. 1963. Reprint, Norman and London: University of Oklahoma Press, 1988.

INDEX

Tugalo River, 60, 85
Tugilo River. *See* Tugalo River.
Tugilo town, 60
Tuskege, 60

Udsidasata. *See* Corn Tassel.
Uku. *See* Old Hop.
Unsuckanail, 74, 80
Upper towns, 19, 27

Valley River, 155, 157
Vann, James, 101-3, 106-7, 108,
    110-12, 113, 114

Wabash, 84
Wafford, James D., 151
Ward, Nancy, 74, 79, 89
War-woman of Chota. *See* Ward,
    Nancy.

Washington, George, 89, 93-94, 98
Water Conjuror. *See* Moytoy.
Watie, Buck. *See* Elias Boudinot.
Watie, Stand, 129
Watoge, 80
Watts, John, 88
Wear's Cove, 99
Wear's Mill, 99
Whatoga, 58
White, Colonel, 91
Willinawaw, 34, 44-47
Will's Town, 115, 117
Will's Valley, 117
Wood-leaning-up. *See* Little
    Carpenter.
Wrosetasatow, 5